AMERICAN BAR

Charles Schumann

AMERICAN BAR

The Artistry of Mixing Drinks

Illustrated by Günter Mattei

ABBEVILLE PRESS PUBLISHERS
NEW YORK   LONDON

CONTENTS

DRINKS AND COCKTAILS FROM A TO Z

COCKTAIL COMPONENTS

THE ARTISTRY OF MIXING DRINKS AND COCKTAILS

Y ou will not find the usual thousand-and-one cocktail recipes in this book. Instead, I have compiled five hundred diverse recipes that strike me as more than sufficient. However, because this book is intended as a reference for bartenders, it naturally includes the best-known indispensable international cocktail recipes.

Here and there I have slightly revised some of the recipes I compiled in *Schumann's Bar Book* and *Tropical Bar Book*. And once again I have retested many standard recipes and occasionally changed them. I always work with certain questions in mind: How much is too much in a cocktail? What does it *not* need? What makes it harmonious? In other words, I always keep in mind the classic three parts of a cocktail: the basis, the modifier, and the flavoring agent.

Browsing through cocktail books, I am often horrified to see recipes calling for an excessive amount of syrups and liqueurs. Sometimes just reading the list of ingredients can make me feel queasy!

In addition, there are a few classic cocktail recipes that I have not included, because I am firmly opposed to the practice of mixing certain spirits. For reasons I explain later, I would never combine gin and vodka, gin and whiskey, vodka and whiskey, gin and brandy, or vodka and brandy.

Because this book is intended for the bartender as well as the general reader, it contains more than just cocktail recipes. I have written also about the bar in general, including bar equipment and cocktails. And a substantial part of the book gives information about the individual components of cocktails, which I consider particularly important. Of course many different interpretations can be found in specialized books in this field. My colleague Stefan Gabányi and the journalist Karl Rudolf contributed significantly in resolving questions and problems I faced while writing this chapter.

I hope that our efforts have resulted in a readable and informative overview of the components of classic cocktail mixing.

Charles Schumann, Munich, May 1995

DRINK INDEX

This index is arranged alphabetically by
1. the most important drink categories
2. the basis spirits

Thus many cocktails appear in two or more categories. The page number indicates the corresponding page in the recipe section.

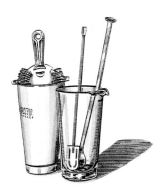

BRANDY DRINKS

CACHAÇA DRINKS

CAMPARI DRINKS

CHAMPAGNE COCKTAILS

CLASSIC DRINKS

COFFEE DRINKS

COLADAS

COLLINSES

DAIQUIRIS

DIGESTIFS

HIGHBALLS

SOURS

TEQUILA DRINKS

24-HOUR DRINKS

VODKA DRINKS

WHISK(E)Y DRINKS

DRINKS AND COCKTAILS FROM A TO Z

1. A date next to the name of a drink indicates this drink was created by the author and the date it was formulated.

2. An asterisk next to the name of a drink refers to a footnote given below.

3. The different glasses that appear with each recipe are my recommendations for serving the drink.

4. "Dash" or "dashes" indicate one or more splashes (the smallest measurement in bartending).

5. "Dry vermouth" refers to dry light vermouth; "vermouth bianco" refers to sweet light vermouth; and "vermouth rosso" refers to sweet dark vermouth.

A

A & B (1982)

1 oz Armagnac
3/4 oz Bénédictine

Stir in an **old-fashioned glass** over ice.

A.C.C. (1983)*

dashes lemon juice
3/4 oz blood orange juice
3/4 oz Wild Turkey
1/4 oz Southern
  Comfort
Champagne

Shake first four ingredients well over ice in a **shaker**, strain into a Champagne flute, fill with Champagne.

American Champagne Cocktail

ABBEY COCKTAIL

1 1/4 oz orange juice
1 1/4 oz gin
dashes orange bitters

Shake over ice in a **shaker** and strain into a cocktail glass.

ABSINTHE SPECIAL

1 $^1/_2$ oz Pernod
dashes anisette
dash orange bitters

Stir in a **small highball glass** over ice, fill with water.

ACAPULCO

$^3/_4$ oz lemon juice
$^3/_4$ oz Rose's lime juice
1 egg white
1 $^1/_2$ oz white rum
dashes Cointreau
lime

Shake well over ice cubes in a **shaker**, strain into a chilled cocktail glass, squeeze an eighth of a lime over the drink and place into the glass.

ADONIS

1 oz dry sherry
$^1/_2$ oz vermouth rosso
$^1/_2$ oz vermouth bianco
dashes orange bitters

Stir well in a **mixing glass** filled with ice cubes, strain into a chilled cocktail glass.

AFFINITY*

¹/₂ oz dry vermouth
¹/₂ oz vermouth rosso
1 oz Scotch
dash orange bitters (or
    Angostura bitters)

Stir well in a **mixing glass**
filled with ice cubes, strain
into a chilled cocktail glass.

Scotch Manhattan

ALASKA

1¹/₂ oz gin
¹/₄ oz yellow Chartreuse
dash orange bitters

Stir well in a **mixing glass**
filled with ice cubes, strain
into a chilled cocktail glass.

ALEXANDER NO. 1

1¹/₂ oz cream
1 oz gin
³/₄ oz crème de cacao
    (white)
nutmeg

Shake well over ice in a
shaker, strain into a cocktail
glass, sprinkle with nutmeg.

Alexandra

ALEXANDER NO. 2

1 1/2 oz cream
1 oz brandy
3/4 oz crème de cacao
   (white)
nutmeg

Shake well over ice in a
shaker, strain into a cocktail
glass, sprinkle with nutmeg.

ALEXANDER'S SISTER

1 1/2 oz cream
1 1/2 oz gin
1/4 oz crème de menthe
   (green)

Shake well over ice in a
shaker, strain into a cocktail
glass.

ALFONSO

1 sugar cube
dashes Angostura bitters
1 1/4 oz Dubonnet
Champagne
lemon twist

Place sugar cube into a
Champagne flute, saturate
with Angostura, add an ice
cube, pour in Dubonnet, fill
with Champagne. Add lemon
twist.

A

AMARETTO & CREAM

1 oz amaretto
1 ½ oz cream

Stir in an **old-fashioned glass** over ice.

AMARETTO SOUR

¾ oz lemon juice
¾ oz orange juice
¾ oz amaretto
stemmed cherry

Shake well over ice in a **shaker**, strain into a sour glass, garnish with cherry.

AMBROSIA

dashes of lemon juice
dashes triple sec
¾ oz brandy
¾ oz Calvados
Champagne

Shake first four ingredients well over ice in a **shaker**, strain into a Champagne flute, fill with Champagne.

AMERICAN BEAUTY

¹/₄ oz dry vermouth
¹/₄ oz vermouth rosso
³/₄ oz brandy
dashes grenadine
³/₄ oz orange juice
tawny port

Stir first five ingredients well over ice in a **mixing glass**, strain into a chilled cocktail glass, float a little port wine on top.

AMERICANO

1 oz Campari
1 oz vermouth rosso (other vermouth may be used)
lemon and orange twists

Pour over ice into an **aperitif glass**, garnish with lemon and orange twists. (May be filled with some club soda.)

ANDALUSIA

1 oz dry sherry
³/₄ oz Spanish brandy
¹/₄ oz white rum
lemon twist

Stir well over ice in a **mixing glass**, strain into chilled cocktail glass, garnish with the twist.

ANGEL FACE

³/₄ oz gin
³/₄ oz brandy
¹/₄ oz apricot brandy

Stir well over ice in a **mixing glass**, strain into chilled cocktail glass.

ANGEL'S DELIGHT

1 ¹/₂ oz cream
dashes grenadine
³/₄ oz triple sec
³/₄ oz gin

Shake well in a **shaker** filled with ice cubes, strain into a cocktail glass.

APEROL SCHUMANN'S (1991)

³/₄ oz lemon juice
³/₄ oz Rose's lime juice
1 ¹/₂ oz Aperol
1 ¹/₄ oz orange juice

Shake well over ice in a **shaker**, strain into a small highball glass over crushed ice, fill with orange juice.

APEROL SOUR

³/₄ oz lemon juice
¹/₄ oz sugar syrup
dash orange bitters
1³/₄ oz Aperol

Shake well over ice in a
shaker, strain into a sour
glass.

APOTHECARY

³/₄ oz Punt e Mes
³/₄ oz Fernet Branca
¹/₄ oz crème de menthe
    (green)

Stir in a **mixing glass** filled
with ice cubes, strain into a
chilled cocktail glass.

APPLE BRANDY HIGHBALL

1³/₄ oz Calvados
soda
apple peel

Pour Calvados into a **collins
glass**, fill with soda, and garnish with apple peel.

A

APPLE BRANDY SOUR

³/₄–1 oz lemon juice
¹/₄–¹/₂ oz sugar syrup
1¹/₄ oz Calvados
stemmed cherry

Shake well over ice in a
shaker, strain into a sour
glass, garnish with cherry.

APPLE CAR

³/₄ oz lemon juice
¹/₄ oz triple sec
1¹/₄ oz Calvados (or
    applejack)
stemmed cherry

Shake well over ice in a
shaker, strain into a sour
glass, garnish with cherry.

APPLE SUNRISE (1980)

dashes lemon juice
¹/₄ oz crème de cassis
1¹/₄ oz Calvados
2³/₄ oz orange juice

Pour each ingredient one
after the other into a **collins
glass**, stir gently.

APPLEJACK HIGHBALL

³/₄ oz orange juice
dashes grenadine
1 ¼ oz Calvados
  (or applejack)
ginger ale

Stir first three ingredients over ice in a **collins glass**, fill with ginger ale.

APRICOT LADY

³/₄ oz lemon juice
1 egg white
³/₄ oz apricot brandy
1 oz white rum
stemmed cherry

Shake well over ice in a **shaker**, strain into a sour glass, garnish with cherry.

APRIL SHOWER

1 oz orange juice
¹/₄ oz Bénédictine
1 oz brandy

Shake over ice in a **shaker**, strain into chilled cocktail glass.

ARTHUR & MARVIN SPECIAL (1985–86)

3½ oz milk
¼ oz lime syrup
¼ oz mango syrup
dashes grenadine
amarelle cherry

Shake well over crushed ice in a **shaker**, strain into a large highball glass, fill with crushed ice, garnish with cherry.

ATTABOY

¼ oz dry vermouth
dash grenadine
1¼ oz gin
lemon twist

Stir well in a **mixing glass** filled with ice cubes, strain into a chilled martini glass, garnish with twist.

AVIATION

¾ oz lemon juice
1 barspoon superfine sugar
dashes maraschino liqueur
1¼ oz gin

Shake well over ice in a **shaker**, strain into a chilled cocktail glass.

B

B & B

1 oz brandy
3/4 oz Bénédictine

Stir over ice cubes in an **old-fashioned glass**. (Can also be served without ice in a sherry glass, in which case it should be prepared in a **mixing glass**.)

B.B.C. (1979)*

1 oz cream
3/4 oz Bénédictine
1 1/4 oz brandy

Stir over ice cubes in an **old-fashioned glass**.

Brandy Bénédictine Cream

B & P

1 oz port (tawny or ruby)
3/4 oz brandy

Stir over ice cubes in an **old-fashioned glass**.

BABYLOVE (1986)

1 $\frac{1}{2}$ oz coconut milk
$\frac{3}{4}$ oz cream
2 oz pineapple juice
$\frac{3}{4}$ oz banana syrup
banana slices

Shake well over crushed ice in a **shaker**, strain into a collins glass, fill with crushed ice, top with banana slices.

BACARDI COCKTAIL

$\frac{3}{4}$ oz lemon or lime juice
1 barspoon powdered sugar
dash grenadine
1$\frac{3}{4}$ oz white Bacardi

Shake well over ice cubes in a **shaker**, strain into a chilled cocktail glass.

BAHIA

2$\frac{3}{4}$–3$\frac{1}{2}$ oz pineapple juice
$\frac{3}{4}$ oz coconut cream
1$\frac{1}{2}$ oz white rum
1 barspoon cream
pineapple chunk
amarelle cherry

Shake well over crushed ice in a **shaker**, strain into a large highball glass half-filled with crushed ice, top with pineapple chunk and amarelle cherry.

BALTIMORE EGGNOG

$^1/_4$ oz cream
1 egg
2 barspoons powdered sugar
$^3/_4$ oz Madeira
$^3/_4$ oz brandy
$^3/_4$ oz dark rum
$2^3/_4$–$3^1/_2$ oz milk

Shake first six ingredients well over ice cubes in a **shaker**, strain into a collins glass over ice cubes, fill with cold milk.

BAMBOO COCKTAIL

1 oz dry sherry
$^3/_4$ oz dry vermouth
dash orange bitters

Stir in a **mixing glass** filled with ice cubes, strain into a chilled cocktail glass.

BANANA DAIQUIRI

juice of a quarter of a lime
$^1/_2$ banana (pureed)
dashes of banana syrup
2 oz white rum

Shake well over ice cubes in a **shaker**, strain into a cocktail glass. (Can also be prepared in a **blender** with crushed ice.)

BARBARA

1 1/2 oz cream
3/4 oz crème de cacao
   (white)
1 1/2 oz vodka
nutmeg

Shake over ice cubes in a
shaker, strain into a cocktail
glass, sprinkle nutmeg on
top.

BATIDA DE BANANA (1986)

1/2 banana
dash banana syrup
1 1/2–2 oz pineapple juice
1/4–3/4 oz cream
3/4 oz cachaça

Prepare in a **blender**, strain
into a large highball glass
over crushed ice.

BATIDA DE COCO (1986)

3/4 oz batida de coco
1/4 oz cream
2 oz pineapple juice
3/4 oz cachaça

Shake well over crushed ice
in a **shaker**, strain into a
large highball glass over
crushed ice.

BATIDA DE MARACUJA (1986)

Chunk of passion fruit
   (or 2 oz maracuja juice)
2 oz pineapple juice
dash lime juice
$^1/_4$ oz lime syrup
$^3/_4$ oz cachaça

Prepare in a **blender**, strain
into a large highball glass
over crushed ice.

BATIDA DO BRAZIL (1986)

$^3/_4$ oz batida de coco
$2^3/_4$ oz coconut milk
$^3/_4$ oz cachaça

Stir over crushed ice in
a **large highball glass**.
(Can also be prepared
in a **shaker**.)

BATIDA DO CARNEVAL (1986)

1 oz orange juice
$2^1/_4$ oz mango juice
$^3/_4$ oz cachaça

Stir well over crushed ice in
a **large highball glass**. (Can
also be prepared in a
shaker.)

BEACHCOMBER

³/₄ oz lime juice
¹/₄ oz triple sec
dash maraschino liqueur
1¹/₂ oz white rum

Shake over ice cubes in a
shaker, strain into chilled
cocktail glass.

BEE'S KISS

³/₄ oz cream
2 barspoons honey
1 oz white rum
¹/₄ oz dark rum

Shake well over ice cubes in
a **shaker**, strain into cocktail
glass.

BELLEVUE (1986)

2 oz pineapple juice
³/₄ oz coconut cream
juice of a quarter lime
¹/₄ oz lime juice
1¹/₂ oz white rum

Shake over ice cubes in a
shaker, strain into a large
highball glass over crushed
ice.

BELLINI*

white peach (pureed)
dashes of lemon juice
dashes of peach brandy
Prosecco or
    Champagne

Stir peach, lemon juice, and brandy in a **Champagne flute**, carefully fill with Prosecco.

Harry's Bar, Venice, house cocktail

BELMONT

1 ½ oz cream
¼ oz raspberry syrup
1 barspoon powdered sugar
1 ½ oz gin

Shake well over ice cubes in a **shaker**, strain into cocktail glass.

BENTLEY

1 oz Dubonnet
1 oz Calvados

Stir over ice in an **old-fashioned glass**.

B

BETWEEN THE SHEETS

$^3/_4$ oz lemon juice
$^1/_4$ oz triple sec
a little powdered sugar
$^3/_4$ oz brandy
$^3/_4$ oz white rum

Shake well over ice cubes in a **shaker**, strain into a chilled cocktail glass.

BIJOU

$^3/_4$ oz dry vermouth
$^1/_4$ oz green Chartreuse
$^3/_4$ oz gin
dash orange bitters

Stir well over ice cubes in a **mixing glass**, strain into a chilled cocktail glass.

BIRD OF PARADISE

$1^1/_2$ oz cream
$^3/_4$ oz crème de cacao
　　(white)
$^1/_4$ oz amaretto
$^3/_4$ oz tequila

Shake over ice cubes in a **shaker**, strain into a cocktail glass.

B

BITTER SWEET

1 oz vermouth rosso
1 oz dry vermouth
dashes of orange bitters
orange peel

Stir in a **mixing glass** filled with ice cubes, strain into a chilled cocktail glass, twist orange peel and add it to the drink.

BITTERS HIGHBALL

dashes of Angostura bitters
(or orange bitters)
ginger ale
lemon peel

Sprinkle dashes of Angostura over ice cubes in a **collins glass**, fill with ginger ale, add lemon peel, stir.

BLACK & FALL

3/4 oz Cognac
3/4 oz Calvados
1/4 oz Cointreau
dashes Pernod

Stir in a **mixing glass** filled with ice cubes, strain into a chilled cocktail glass.

BLACK DEVIL*

¹/₄ oz dry vermouth
2 oz white rum
black olive

Stir in a mixing glass filled with ice cubes, strain into a chilled martini glass, add black olive. (Can also be stirred over ice cubes in an old-fashioned glass.)

Rum Martini

BLACK JACK

³/₄ oz brandy
³/₄ oz kirschwasser
1 cup cold coffee
sugar (if desired)

Stir over ice cubes in a small highball glass.

BLACK MAGIC

1 oz vodka
¹/₄ oz Kahlúa
1 cup cold coffee
dashes of lemon juice

Stir over ice cubes in a small highball glass.

BLACK MARIA

1 oz dark rum
3/4 oz Tia Maria
1 barspoon sugar
1 cup cold coffee
lemon peel

Stir over ice cubes in a **small highball glass**, twist the lemon peel and drop into the glass.

BLACK MARIE (1986)

3/4 oz dark rum
3/4 oz brandy
1/4 oz Tia Maria
1 cup cold coffee
1 barspoon brown
   sugar

Shake well over crushed ice in a **shaker**, strain into a large highball glass.

BLACK RUSSIAN

1 1/2 oz vodka
3/4 oz Kahlúa

Stir over ice cubes in an **old-fashioned glass**.

BLACK VELVET

Guinness
Champagne

Fill a **Champagne flute** half-way with Guinness, carefully top with Champagne.

BLACK WIDOW

juice of half a lime
1 barspoon powdered sugar
¼ oz Southern Comfort
1 oz gold rum

Shake well over ice cubes in a **shaker**, strain into a sour glass.

BLACKTHORN

¾ oz Noilly Prat
¾ oz Irish whiskey
dash anisette
dash Angostura bitters

Stir in a **mixing glass** filled with ice cubes, strain into a chilled cocktail glass.

B

BLANCHE

1 oz triple sec
$^1/_4$ oz anisette
dashes of lemon juice

Shake over crushed ice in a
shaker, strain into a chilled
cocktail glass.

BLOOD AND SAND COCKTAIL

1 $^1/_2$ oz orange juice
$^1/_4$ oz cherry brandy
$^3/_4$ oz vermouth rosso
$^3/_4$ oz Scotch

Shake over ice cubes in a
shaker, strain into a chilled
cocktail glass.

BLOODHOUND COCKTAIL

$^3/_4$ oz dry vermouth
$^3/_4$ oz vermouth bianco
$^3/_4$ oz gin

Stir over ice cubes in a
mixing glass, strain into a
chilled cocktail glass.

BLOODY BULL

¹/₄ oz lemon juice
celery salt
ground pepper, Tabasco,
    Worcestershire sauce
1¹/₂ oz vodka
2 oz tomato juice
2 oz bouillon
celery stalk

Stir well over ice cubes in a **collins glass.** Garnish with celery stalk. (Can also be prepared in a **shaker.**)

BLOODY MARIA*

¹/₄ oz lemon juice
Worcestershire sauce
celery salt
ground pepper
Tabasco
1¹/₂ oz tequila
4 oz tomato juice
celery stalk

Stir well over ice cubes in a **collins glass.** Garnish with celery stalk. (Can also be prepared in a **shaker.**)

* Tequila Maria

BLOODY MARY

¹/₄ oz lemon juice
Worcestershire sauce
celery salt
ground pepper, Tabasco
1¹/₂ oz vodka
4 oz tomato juice
celery stalk

Stir well over ice cubes in a **collins glass.** Garnish with celery stalk.

BLOODY VIRGIN BULL

2 oz tomato juice
2 oz bouillon
$^1/_4$ oz lemon juice
Worcestershire sauce
celery salt
ground pepper
Tabasco

Stir over ice cubes in a
collins glass.

BLUE CHAMPAGNE

$^1/_4$ oz lemon juice
dashes triple sec
dashes blue curaçao
1 oz vodka (or gin)
Champagne

Shake first four ingredients
over ice cubes in a **shaker**,
strain into a Champagne
flute, fill with Champagne.

BLUE DEVIL

$^1/_4$ oz lemon juice
dashes maraschino liqueur
dashes blue curaçao
a little powdered sugar
1 oz gin

Shake well over ice cubes in
a **shaker**, strain into a cocktail glass.

BLUE MOON

1 1/2 oz cream
dashes Galliano
1/4 oz blue curaçao
3/4 oz tequila

Shake over ice cubes in a **shaker**, strain into a cocktail glass.

BOBBY BURNS*

3/4 oz vermouth rosso
3/4 oz dry vermouth
3/4 oz Scotch
dash Bénédictine
stemmed cherry

Stir in a **mixing glass** filled with ice cubes, strain into a chilled cocktail glass. Garnish with cherry.

Rob Roy variation

BOINA ROJA (RED BERET)

juice of half a lime
dashes of grenadine
1 barspoon powdered sugar
3/4 oz white rum
1 1/4 oz white rum
    (extra aged)
mint sprig
stemmed cherry

Stir well over crushed ice in a **small highball glass**, add squeezed lime, garnish with mint sprig and cherry. (May also be prepared in a **shaker**.)

BOLERO

³/₄ oz vermouth rosso
³/₄ oz white rum
³/₄ oz Calvados (or apple brandy)

Stir over ice cubes in a **mixing glass**, strain into a chilled cocktail glass.

BOMBAY

¹/₂ oz dry vermouth
¹/₂ oz vermouth bianco
³/₄ oz brandy
dash Pernod

Stir over ice cubes in a **mixing glass**, strain into a chilled cocktail glass.

BORIS'S GOOD NIGHT CUP (1986)

³/₄ oz cream
half a banana
dashes of banana syrup
1¹/₂ oz pineapple juice
1¹/₂ oz papaya juice

Prepare in a **blender** with crushed ice, strain into a large highball glass.

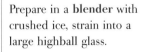

B

BOSTON SOUR

3/4 oz lemon juice
1 egg white
2 barspoons powdered sugar
dashes sugar syrup
1 1/2 oz Bourbon
stemmed cherry

Shake well over ice cubes in a **shaker**, strain into an old-fashioned glass over ice cubes, garnish with cherry.

BOURBON HIGHBALL

2 oz Bourbon
ginger ale
spiral lemon twist

Pour Bourbon over ice cubes in a **collins glass** with ginger ale, add the spiral lemon twist. (Other sodas or water can be used in mixing this drink.)

BRANDY ALEXANDER

1 oz cream
2 teaspoons whipped cream
3/4 oz crème de cacao
   (brown)
1 oz brandy
nutmeg

Shake well over ice cubes in a **shaker**, strain into a cock-tail glass, sprinkle with nutmeg.

BRANDY & SODA*

$1^3/_4$–2 oz brandy
soda

Pour brandy over ice cubes into a **collins glass** with soda. (In the Far East premium Cognacs are used.)

Fine à l'eau

BRANDY EGGNOG

1 egg yolk
$^1/_4$ oz sugar syrup
$1^1/_2$ oz brandy
$^1/_4$ oz tawny port
$3^1/_2$ oz milk
$^3/_4$ oz cream
nutmeg

Shake well over ice cubes in a **shaker**, strain into a large highball glass over ice cubes, sprinkle with nutmeg.

BRANDY FLIP

1 egg yolk
$^1/_4$ oz sugar syrup
$^3/_4$ oz cream
$1^3/_4$ oz brandy
nutmeg

Shake well over ice cubes in a **shaker**, strain into a cocktail glass, sprinkle with nutmeg.

B

BRANDY SOUR

³/₄ oz lemon juice
¹/₄–³/₄ oz sugar syrup
1¹/₂ oz brandy
stemmed cherry

Shake well over ice cubes in a **shaker**, strain into a sour glass, garnish with cherry.

BRANDY STINGER

1¹/₂ oz brandy
³/₄ oz crème de menthe
(white)

Stir over ice cubes in an **old-fashioned glass**.

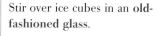

BRAVE BULL

1 oz tequila
³/₄ oz Tia Maria
whipped cream

Stir tequila and Tia Maria over ice cubes in a **mixing glass**, strain into a chilled sherry glass, top with whipped cream.

B

BRAZIL

1 oz dry vermouth
1 oz dry sherry
dashes Pernod

Stir well over ice cubes in a
mixing glass, strain into a
chilled cocktail glass.

BREAKFAST EGGNOG

1 egg
1 barspoon powdered sugar
$^1/_4$ oz triple sec
$^3/_4$ oz apricot brandy
2 oz milk
$^1/_4$ oz cream
nutmeg

Shake well over ice cubes in
a **shaker**, strain into a cocktail glass, sprinkle with
nutmeg.

BRIGHTON PUNCH

$^3/_4$ oz lemon juice
$^1/_4$ oz Bénédictine
1 barspoon powdered sugar
$^3/_4$ oz brandy
$^3/_4$ oz Bourbon
2 oz orange juice

Shake over ice cubes in a
shaker, strain into a collins
glass over ice cubes.

B

BRIGITTE BARDOT (1981)

3/4 oz cream
1 egg yolk
1/4 oz sugar syrup
3/4 oz brandy
1/4 oz Bourbon

Shake over ice cubes in a **shaker**, strain into a cocktail glass.

BROKEN SPUR COCKTAIL

1 egg yolk
3/4 oz vermouth bianco
dashes anisette
3/4 oz gin
3/4 oz white port

Shake well over ice cubes in a **shaker**, strain into a cocktail glass.

BRONX MEDIUM (PERFECT)

1/4 oz vermouth rosso
1/4 oz dry vermouth
1 oz gin
1 1/2 oz orange juice

Shake over ice cubes in a **shaker**, strain into a chilled cocktail glass.
Dry: use only dry vermouth
Sweet: use only vermouth rosso

B

BRONX GOLDEN

with 1 egg yolk	Prepare the same as a Bronx Medium.

BRONX SILVER

with 1 egg white	Prepare the same as a Bronx Medium.

BROOKLYN

3/4 oz vermouth rosso 1 oz rye whiskey dashes maraschino liqueur	Stir well in a **mixing glass** filled with ice cubes, strain into a chilled cocktail glass.

B

BROWN FOX

1 1/2 oz Bourbon
3/4 oz Bénédictine

Stir over ice cubes in an **old-fashioned glass**.

BUCKS FIZZ

2 oz orange juice
Champagne

Pour orange juice over ice cubes in a **Champagne flute**, fill with Champagne, stir gently.

BULLDOG HIGHBALL

1 1/2 oz orange juice
1 1/2 oz gin
ginger ale

Stir juice and gin over ice cubes in a **collins glass**, fill with ginger ale.

B

BULLFROG

1 ½ oz vodka
Seven-Up
lime

Pour vodka over ice cubes in a **collins glass**, fill with Seven-Up, squeeze a lime wedge into drink and drop into the glass; stir gently.

BULLSHOT

1 ¾–2 oz vodka
3 ½ oz beef bouillon

Stir vodka and cold beef bouillon in a **small highball glass**. (Prepare the bouillon with a lot of celery and taste-test it while cooking–not after!)

BULL'S MILK

1 ½ oz dark rum
¾ oz Cognac
milk
maple syrup

Heat liquors in a **heat-resistant glass**, fill with hot milk, sweeten with maple syrup. (Can also be served cold.)

B

BUNUELONI

1 oz Punt e Mes
1 oz vermouth bianco
3/4 oz gin
lemon and orange peels

Stir over ice cubes in an
aperitif or **highball glass**,
twist lemon and orange
peels over the glass and drop
into the glass.

BUSHRANGER

1 oz Dubonnet
1 oz white rum
dashes of Angostura bitters

Stir over ice cubes in an **old-fashioned glass**.

C. C.*

1–1¼ oz Campari
Champagne
lemon peel

Pour Campari into a **Champagne flute**, fill with Champagne, twist lemon peel over drink.

Campari Champagne

CAFÉ BRÙLOT

1–1½ oz Cognac
dashes triple sec
1 cup hot coffee
lemon and orange peels
clove
cinnamon
sugar cube

Warm Cognac in a **heat-resistant glass**, pour in hot coffee, add lemon and orange peels, clove, and cinnamon, stir, and add sugar cube.

CAFÉ CAEN (1983)

1 oz Calvados
¼–¾ oz Grand Marnier
1 cup hot coffee
lightly whipped cream
sugar cube

Heat liquors in a **heat-resistant glass**, pour in coffee, stir, top with cream, add sugar cube.

CAFÉ DE PARIS

1 oz cream
1 egg white
½ oz anisette
1 barspoon powdered sugar
1 oz gin

Shake over ice cubes in a **shaker**, strain into a cocktail glass.

CAFÉ PUCCI (1983)

1 oz gold rum
¼ oz amaretto
brown sugar
1 cup espresso
lightly whipped
    cream

Warm liquors in a **heat-resistant glass**, stir in sugar, pour in espresso, stir again, top with cream.

C

CAFÉ SAN JUAN (1983)

1 ½ oz gold rum
1 cup strong cold coffee
lemon peel
sugar

Pour rum over ice cubes into a **small highball glass**, fill with coffee, stir. Twist lemon peel over drink and drop into the glass, add sugar.

CAIPIRINHA

lime
2 oz cachaça
1–2 barspoons sugar (or sugar cubes)

Place lime wedge and sugar into a **small highball glass**, press well with a pestle, pour in cachaça, stir. Fill with crushed ice and stir again.

CAIPIRISSIMA

with 1 ½ oz white rum

Prepare the same as Caipirinha.

CAIPIROSKA

with 1 ½ oz vodka

Prepare the same as Caipirinha.

Cachaça Nega Fula

CALEDONIA

¾ oz milk
¾ oz cream
1 egg yolk
¾ oz crème de cacao
   (brown)
¾ oz brandy

Shake well over ice cubes in a **shaker**, strain into a cocktail glass.

CAMPARI COCKTAIL

1 oz Campari
¾ oz vodka
dash Angostura bitters
lemon peel

Shake well over ice in a **shaker**, strain into a chilled cocktail glass, twist lemon peel over drink and drop into the glass.

CAMPARI ORANGE

1½ oz Campari
orange juice

Pour Campari over ice into a **collins glass** and fill with orange juice.

CAMPARI SHAKERATO

dashes of lemon juice
1 1/2–1 3/4 oz Campari
lemon peel

Shake well over crushed ice in a **shaker**, strain into a chilled aperitif or cocktail glass, twist lemon peel over drink and drop into the glass.

CARABINIERI

1/4 oz lime juice
1/4 oz Rose's lime juice
1 egg yolk
1/4 oz Galliano
1 barspoon powdered sugar
1 oz tequila
2 oz orange juice

Shake well over ice cubes in a **shaker**, strain into a small highball glass over crushed ice.

CARDINAL*

3/4 oz dry vermouth
3/4 oz Campari
3/4 oz gin
lemon peel

Stir over ice cubes in an **aperitif glass**, twist lemon peel over drink and drop into the glass. (Can be filled with soda.)

Negroni variation

CARL JOSEF (1983)

³/₄ oz kirschwasser
¹/₄ oz cherry liqueur (Cherry
  Heering)
Champagne

Stir kirschwasser and cherry liqueur in a **mixing glass** filled with ice cubes, strain into a Champagne flute, fill with Champagne.

CARUSO

³/₄ oz dry vermouth
³/₄ oz gin
¹/₄ oz crème de menthe
  (green)

Stir well over ice cubes in a **mixing glass**, strain into a chilled cocktail glass. (Can also be stirred and served in an **old-fashioned glass**.)

CASABLANCA

¹/₄ oz lemon juice
³/₄ oz egg liqueur
  (advocaat)
1¹/₂ oz orange juice
1 oz vodka

Shake well over ice cubes in a **shaker**, strain into cocktail glass.

CASINO

1 ½ oz gin
dashes lemon juice
dash maraschino liqueur
dash orange bitters

Stir well over ice cubes in a **mixing glass**, strain into a chilled martini glass.

CASTRO COOLER

¾ oz lime juice
¾ oz Rose's lime juice
1 ½ oz orange juice
1 barspoon powdered sugar
1 ½ oz gold rum
¾ oz Calvados
lime

Shake well over crushed ice in a **shaker**, strain into a collins glass over crushed ice, squeeze lime wedge over drink and drop into the glass.

CENTENARIO

juice of a lime
dash grenadine
¼ oz Tia Maria
¼ oz triple sec
¾ oz white rum
  (extra aged)
1 ½ oz gold rum
mint sprig

Stir well over crushed ice in a **collins glass**, garnish with mint sprig.

C

CHAMPAGNE COCKTAIL

1 sugar cube
dashes Angostura bitters
Champagne
lemon peel
orange

Place sugar cube into a **Champagne flute** and saturate with Angostura, pour in Champagne, twist lemon peel over drink and drop it into the glass along with an orange wedge.

CHAMPAGNE FLIP

1 egg yolk
$^1/_4$ oz sugar syrup
$^1/_4$ oz cream
dashes Cointreau
$^3/_4$ oz brandy
Champagne
nutmeg

Shake first five ingredients well over ice cubes in a **shaker**, strain into a Champagne flute, carefully fill with Champagne, and sprinkle with nutmeg.

CHAPALA

$^3/_4$ oz lemon juice
dash grenadine
dash triple sec
$1^1/_2$ oz tequila
$1^1/_2$–2 oz orange juice

Stir over crushed ice in a **collins glass**.

CHARLES'S CARIBBEAN (1980)

dashes lemon juice
1 1/2 oz orange juice
1 1/2 oz maracuja juice
3/4 oz cream
3/4 oz coconut cream
1 oz white rum
3/4 oz dark rum
pineapple, stemmed cherry

Shake well over crushed ice in a **shaker**, strain into a collins glass over ice, add pineapple chunks and cherry.

CHARLES'S DAIQUIRI (1980)

3/4 oz lime juice
1/4–3/4 oz sugar syrup
1 barspoon powdered sugar
1 1/2 oz white rum
1/4 oz dark rum
dashes Cointreau

Shake well over ice cubes in a **shaker**, strain into a chilled cocktail glass.

CHERRY BLOSSOM

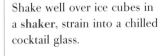

3/4 oz lemon juice
1/4 oz cherry brandy
dash grenadine
1 oz brandy

Shake well over ice cubes in a **shaker**, strain into a chilled cocktail glass.

CHERRY FIZZ

3/4–1 oz lemon juice
3/4 oz cherry brandy
3/4 oz brandy
soda
cherry juice

Shake first three ingredients well over ice cubes in a **shaker**, strain into a collins glass over ice cubes, fill with soda, add a little cherry juice.

CHERRY FLIP

1 egg yolk
1 barspoon powdered sugar
3/4 oz cherry brandy
3/4 oz brandy
3/4 oz cream

Shake well over ice cubes in a **shaker**, strain into a cocktail glass.

CHI CHI

1 1/2 oz pineapple juice
3/4 oz coconut cream
3/4 oz cream
2 oz vodka
pineapple chunk
amarelle cherry

Shake well over crushed ice in a **shaker**, strain into a large highball glass filled with crushed ice, serve with pineapple chunk and amarelle cherry.

CHICAGO FIZZ

³/₄ oz lemon juice
1 egg white
1 barspoon powdered sugar
³/₄ oz ruby port
³/₄ oz white rum
soda

Shake first five ingredients well over ice cubes in a **shaker**, strain into a collins glass over ice cubes, fill with soda.

CHOCO COLADA (1982)

³/₄ oz cream
1 ¹/₂ oz milk
¹/₄ oz coconut cream
³/₄ oz chocolate syrup
¹/₄ oz Tia Maria
1 oz white rum
³/₄ oz dark rum
bitter chocolate

Shake liquids well over crushed ice in a **shaker**, strain into a large highball glass over crushed ice, grate chocolate on top.

CLAMATO COCKTAIL

2 oz tomato juice, spiced
2 oz clam juice, spiced
1 ¹/₂ oz vodka

Stir well over ice cubes in a **small highball glass**.

CLARIDGE

³/₄ oz dry vermouth
dash apricot brandy
dash triple sec
³/₄ oz gin
lemon peel

Stir in a **mixing glass** filled with ice cubes, strain into a chilled cocktail glass, twist lemon peel over drink and drop into the glass.

CLOVER CLUB*

³/₄ oz lemon juice
1 egg white
dash grenadine
1 barspoon sugar
1¹/₂ oz gin

Shake well over ice cubes in a **shaker**, strain into a chilled cocktail glass.

Pink Lady

COCO CHOCO (1982)

3¹/₂ oz milk
³/₄ oz cream
³/₄ oz coconut cream
³/₄–1 oz chocolate syrup
bitter chocolate

Shake liquids well over ice cubes in a **shaker**, strain into a large highball glass over crushed ice, grate chocolate on top.

COCONUT BANANA (1982)

2 oz milk
³/₄ oz cream
³/₄ oz coconut cream
³/₄ oz banana syrup (or half
a banana pureed
in a blender)

Shake well over ice cubes in
a **shaker**, strain into a large
highball glass over crushed
ice.

COCONUT DREAM

1¹/₂ oz cream
¹/₄ oz coconut cream
¹/₄ oz banana liqueur
³/₄ oz crème de cacao
(white)

Shake well over ice cubes in
a **shaker**, strain into a cocktail glass.

COCONUT KISS (1986)

1 oz cream
³/₄ oz coconut cream
1¹/₂ oz cherry juice
dash grenadine
1¹/₂ oz pineapple
juice
amarelle cherry

Shake over ice cubes in a
shaker, strain into a large
highball glass over crushed
ice, garnish with amarelle
cherry.

C

COCONUT LIPS (1982)

2 oz pineapple juice
1 1/2 oz cream
1/4–3/4 oz coconut cream
1/4 oz raspberry syrup
pineapple chunk
amarelle cherry

Shake well over ice cubes in a **shaker**, strain into a large highball glass over crushed ice, add pineapple chunk and amarelle cherry.

COLADA BRAZIL (1986)

3/4 oz cream
3/4 oz coconut cream
2 oz pineapple juice
3/4 oz white rum
1 1/2 oz cachaça

Prepare with crushed ice in a **shaker** or a **blender**, pour into a large highball glass over crushed ice.

COLIBRI

2 3/4 oz orange juice
1 oz white rum
3/4 oz dark rum
dashes Angostura bitters

Shake well over ice cubes in a **shaker**, strain into a large highball glass over crushed ice.

COLUMBUS COCKTAIL

juice of a lime
³/₄ oz apricot brandy
1¹/₂ oz gold rum

Shake well over ice cubes in a **shaker**, strain into a chilled cocktail glass.

CONTINENTAL

¹/₂ lime
1 barspoon powdered sugar
1¹/₂ oz white rum
¹/₄ oz crème de menthe
   (green)

Squeeze lime into a **small highball glass**, add sugar and rum, stir, fill with crushed ice, add crème de menthe, stir again.

COOPERSTOWN

³/₄ oz dry vermouth
³/₄ oz vermouth rosso
³/₄ oz gin

Stir in a **mixing glass** filled with ice cubes, strain into a chilled cocktail glass.

COPACABANA (1986)

¾ oz cream
1½ oz papaya juice
¾ oz pineapple juice
¾ oz chocolate syrup
1¾ oz cachaça

Shake well over ice cubes in a **shaker**, strain into a large highball glass, fill with crushed ice.

CORONATION

¾ oz Dubonnet
¾ oz dry vermouth
¾ oz gin

Stir in a **mixing glass** filled with ice cubes, strain into a chilled cocktail glass.

CORPSE REVIVER No. 1*

3/4 oz vermouth rosso
3/4 oz Calvados
   (or applejack)
3/4 oz brandy

Stir well over ice cubes in a **mixing glass**, strain into a cocktail glass, serve with a glass of ice water.

Frank Meier, Ritz Bar, Paris

CORPSE REVIVER No. 2*

3/4 oz Pernod
Champagne
lemon juice

Pour Pernod into a **Champagne flute**, fill with Champagne, sprinkle with a little lemon juice.

Frank Meier, Ritz Bar, Paris

CORPSE REVIVER No. 3

3/4 oz brandy
3/4 oz Fernet Branca
3/4 oz crème de menthe
   (white)

Stir over ice cubes in a **mixing glass**, strain into a chilled cocktail glass, serve with a glass of ice water.

CRÈME DE MENTHE FRAPPÉ

$^3/_4$ oz peppermint syrup

Pour over crushed ice into a **small highball glass**, fill with crushed ice, serve with two short straws and a carafe of ice water.

CREOLE

dash lemon juice
salt
ground pepper (coarse)
Worcestershire sauce
Tabasco
$1^1/_2$ oz white rum
$3^1/_2$ oz beef bouillon

Stir over ice cubes in a **collins glass**

CUBA LIBRE

lime
$1^1/_2$–2 oz white rum
cola

Squeeze lime wedge into a **collins glass** and drop it into the glass, add ice cubes, pour in rum, fill with cola, stir.

C

CUBAN HOT COFFEE (1986)

1 oz gold rum
$^1\!/_4$ oz crème de cacao
    (brown)
1 barspoon sugar
1 cup hot coffee

Heat liquors in a **heat-resistant glass**, add sugar, fill with coffee, and stir.

CUBAN ISLAND (1984)

$^3\!/_4$ oz lemon juice
$^1\!/_4$–$^3\!/_4$ oz Cointreau
$^3\!/_4$ oz vodka
$^3\!/_4$ oz white rum

Shake well over ice cubes in a **shaker**, strain into a chilled cocktail glass.

CUBAN MANHATTAN

$^3\!/_4$ oz dry vermouth
$^3\!/_4$ oz vermouth rosso
1 oz white rum
dashes Angostura bitters
stemmed cherry

Stir well over ice cubes in a **mixing glass**, strain into a chilled cocktail glass, add cherry.

CUBAN SPECIAL

juice of half a lime
¼ oz triple sec
¼ oz pineapple juice
1½ oz white rum

Shake well over ice cubes in a **shaker**, strain into a chilled cocktail glass.

CYNAR COCKTAIL

1 oz vermouth bianco
1 oz Cynar
orange

Stir over ice cubes in an **aperitif glass**, squeeze orange wedge over drink and drop it into the glass.

D

DAIQUIRI NATURAL*

¾ oz lime juice
¼–½ oz sugar syrup
2 oz white rum

Shake well over ice cubes in a **shaker**, strain into a chilled cocktail glass.

*original version from 1898

DEAUVILLE

¾ oz lemon juice
1 barspoon powdered sugar
¼–¾ oz triple sec
¾ oz Calvados
¾ oz brandy

Shake well over ice cubes in a **shaker**, strain into a chilled cocktail glass.

DEEP-SEA DIVER

juice of a lime
¼ oz lime syrup
1 barspoon powdered sugar
¾ oz triple sec
¾ oz white rum
2 oz dark rum
2 oz high-proof
   dark rum

Shake well over crushed ice in a **shaker**, strain into a large highball glass over crushed ice, drop squeezed lime into glass.

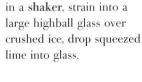

DEEP SOUTH (1982)

¹/₄ oz lemon juice
¹/₄ oz Rose's lime juice
¹/₄ oz dark rum
¹/₄ oz Southern
    Comfort
Champagne

Shake first four ingredients
well over ice cubes in a
shaker, strain into a Champagne flute, fill with Champagne.

DERBY

1¹/₂ oz gin
dash Peychaud bitters

Stir over ice cubes in a
mixing glass, strain into a
sherry glass.

DERBY DAIQUIRI

juice of a quarter lime
³/₄ oz orange juice
1 barspoon powdered sugar
2 oz white rum

Shake well over ice cubes in
a **shaker**, strain into a chilled
cocktail glass.

DEVIL

¾ oz dry vermouth
1 oz tawny port
dash lemon juice
lemon peel

Stir well over ice cubes in a **mixing glass**, strain into a chilled cocktail glass, twist lemon peel over drink and drop it into the glass.

DIPLOMAT

¾ oz dry vermouth
¾ oz vermouth rosso
dash maraschino liqueur
dash orange bitters
lemon peel
stemmed cherry

Stir well over ice cubes in a **mixing glass**, strain into a chilled cocktail glass, twist lemon peel over drink and drop it into the glass, garnish with cherry.

DIRTY MOTHER

1 oz brandy
¾ oz Kahlúa

Stir over ice cubes in a **small highball glass**.

DIRTY WHITE MOTHER

with 1 oz cream

Prepare the same as a Dirty Mother, add cream.

D

DUBONNET CASSIS

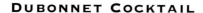

1¾ oz Dubonnet
¼ oz crème de cassis
soda
lemon peel

Stir Dubonnet and cassis over ice cubes in an **aperitif glass**, fill with soda, twist lemon peel over drink and drop it into the glass.

DUBONNET COCKTAIL

1 oz Dubonnet
¾ oz gin
dash orange bitters
lemon peel

Stir in a **mixing glass** filled with ice cubes, strain into a chilled cocktail glass, twist lemon peel over drink and drop it into the glass.

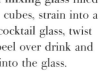

DUBONNET FIZZ

¾ oz lemon juice
1 barspoon powdered sugar
1½ oz orange juice
1¾ oz Dubonnet
soda
stemmed cherry

Shake first four ingredients well over ice cubes in a **shaker**, strain into a collins glass over ice cubes, fill with soda, add cherry.

D

DUBONNET HIGHBALL

1³/₄ oz Dubonnet
ginger ale
spiral lemon peel

Pour Dubonnet over ice
cubes into a **collins glass**, fill
with ginger ale, add spiral
lemon peel.

DUE CAMPARI (1988)

³/₄ oz lemon juice
³/₄ oz Cordial Campari
¹/₄ oz Campari
Prosecco or
    Champagne

Shake lemon juice and
Campari well over ice cubes
in a **shaker**, strain into a
Champagne flute, fill with
Prosecco.

DUKE OF MARLBORO

1 oz dry sherry
1 oz vermouth rosso
dash orange bitters
orange peel

Stir well over ice cubes in a
mixing glass, strain into a
chilled cocktail glass, twist
orange peel over drink and
drop it into the glass.

E

EAST INDIA*

1¹/₂ oz pineapple juice
dash Angostura bitters
1¹/₂ oz brandy

Shake well over ice cubes in a **shaker**, strain into a small highball glass over ice cubes.

Frank Meier, Ritz Bar, Paris

EAST INDIAN

1 oz dry sherry
³/₄ oz dry vermouth
¹/₄ oz vermouth bianco
dash orange bitters

Stir in a **mixing glass** filled with ice cubes, strain into a chilled cocktail glass.

EASTWIND

³/₄ oz vermouth rosso
³/₄ oz dry vermouth
³/₄ oz vodka
orange, lemon

Stir over ice cubes in an **aperitif glass**, add orange and lemon slices.

E

EGG SOUR

¹/₄ oz lemon juice
1 barspoon powdered sugar
1 egg yolk
³/₄ oz triple sec
1 oz brandy
stemmed cherry

Shake well over ice cubes in a **shaker**, strain into an old-fashioned glass over ice cubes (or into a sour glass without ice), add cherry.

EL DIABLO

2 oz tequila
¹/₄–³/₄ oz crème de cassis
ginger ale
lime

Stir tequila and cassis over ice cubes in a **collins glass**, fill with ginger ale, squeeze lime wedge over drink and drop it into the glass.

EL PRESIDENTE

³/₄ oz dry vermouth
¹/₄ oz vermouth rosso
dash grenadine
¹/₄ oz triple sec
1¹/₂ oz white rum
dash lemon juice

Stir in a **mixing glass** filled with ice, strain into a chilled cocktail glass.

ERNEST HEMINGWAY SPECIAL

juice of half a lime
$^1/_4$–$^3/_4$ oz grapefruit juice
$^1/_4$ oz maraschino liqueur
1$^1/_2$ oz white rum

Shake well over ice cubes in a **shaker**, strain into a chilled cocktail glass.

EYE-OPENER

1 egg yolk
1 barspoon powdered sugar
$^1/_4$ oz crème de cacao
   (white)
dash anisette
1 oz white rum

Shake well in a **shaker** filled with ice cubes, strain into a cocktail glass.

FALLEN ANGEL

dash lemon juice
dash crème de menthe
   (white)
$1^{1}/_{2}$ oz gin
dash Angostura bitters

Shake over ice cubes in a
shaker, strain into a chilled
cocktail glass.

FALLEN LEAVES (1982)

$3/_4$ oz vermouth rosso
$^{1}/_{4}$ oz dry vermouth
$3/_4$ oz Calvados
dash brandy
lemon peel

Stir in a **mixing glass** filled
with ice cubes, strain into a
chilled cocktail glass, twist
lemon peel over drink and
drop it into the glass.

FAT SAILOR

juice of half a lime
$1^{1}/_{4}$ oz Rose's lime juice
$^{1}/_{4}$ oz Tia Maria
$3/_4$ oz white rum
$1^{1}/_{4}$ oz dark rum
$1^{1}/_{4}$ oz high-proof
   dark rum

Shake well over crushed ice
in a **shaker**, strain into a
large highball glass over
crushed ice, drop the
squeezed lime into the glass.

FERRARI

2 oz dry vermouth
dash amaretto

Stir over ice cubes in a **small highball glass.**

FIESTA

dash lime juice
dash grenadine
³/₄ oz Noilly Prat
³/₄ oz Calvados
³/₄ oz white rum

Stir over ice cubes in a **mixing glass**, strain into a chilled cocktail glass.

FIFTH AVENUE

1 ¹/₂ oz cream
³/₄ oz crème de cacao
    (white)
³/₄ oz apricot brandy

Shake over ice cubes in a **shaker**, strain into a cocktail glass.

FINO MARTINI

dashes fino sherry
1 1/2 oz gin
lemon peel

Stir well over ice cubes in a **mixing glass**, strain into a chilled martini glass, twist lemon peel over drink and drop it into the glass.

FIREMAN'S SOUR

3/4 oz lime juice
1 barspoon powdered sugar
dash grenadine
1 oz white rum
1/4 oz dark rum
lime

Shake well over ice cubes in a **shaker**, strain into a small highball glass over crushed ice, squeeze lime wedge over drink and drop it into the drink.

FISH HOUSE PUNCH No. 1

5 liters (5 qts, 8 oz) water
500 grams (1 lb., 4 oz)
  brown sugar
3 liters (4 750-ml bottles)
  dark rum
1 liter (1 750-ml bottle,
  8 oz) brandy
¼ liter (8 oz) Southern
  Comfort
juice of 10 limes
lime peels

Heat water, stir in sugar, allow to boil. Add liquors, stir well, simmer. Stir in lime juice and peels. Serve hot in heat-resistant glasses. (Or cool and bottle. Sealed bottles can be kept for a long period.) If served cold, pour into a large highball glass over crushed ice, sprinkle with a little dark rum.

FISH HOUSE PUNCH No. 2*

2 liters (2 qts, 3½ oz) water
3 liters (3 qts, 5½ oz) black
  tea
honey
sugar syrup
2 liters (2 750-ml bottles,
  16 oz) dark rum
½ liter (16 oz) brandy
juice of 5 limes
lime peels

Prepare the same as Fish House Punch No. 1, sweeten to taste.

Schumann's version

FLAMINGO

juice of a quarter lime
dashes grenadine
1 oz pineapple juice
1½ oz white rum

Shake over crushed ice in a
shaker, strain into a cocktail
glass.

FLORIDA DAIQUIRI

juice of half a lime
1 barspoon sugar
¼ oz grapefruit juice
¼ oz maraschino liqueur
2 oz white rum

Shake over crushed ice in a
shaker, strain into a cocktail
glass.

FLORIDA SLING

¾ oz lemon juice
1 barspoon powdered sugar
dash grenadine
1½ oz pineapple juice
1½ oz gin
¼–¾ oz cherry
    brandy
stemmed cherry

Shake well over ice cubes in
a **shaker**, strain into a collins
glass half-filled with crushed
ice, garnish with cherry.

F

FLORIDA SPECIAL

¾ oz orange juice
¼ oz maraschino liqueur
¼ oz red curaçao
    (or triple sec)
1½ oz gold rum

Shake over crushed ice in a **shaker**, strain into a chilled cocktail glass.

FLYING

¾ oz lemon juice
1 barspoon powdered sugar
¼ oz triple sec
¾ oz gin
Champagne

Shake first four ingredients well over ice cubes in a **shaker**, strain into a Champagne flute, fill with Champagne.

FLYING DUTCHMAN

1½ oz gin
dash triple sec
lime

Stir over ice cubes in a **small highball glass**, squeeze a lime wedge over drink and drop it into the drink.

F

FLYING KANGAROO (1979)

¹/₄ oz cream
³/₄ oz coconut cream
1¹/₂ oz pineapple juice
³/₄ oz orange juice
¹/₄ oz Galliano
1 oz vodka
1 oz white rum
pineapple

Shake well over ice cubes in a **shaker**, strain into a large highball glass with crushed ice, add pineapple chunks.

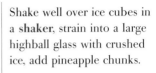

FOGGY DAY (1980)

1¹/₂ oz gin
¹/₄ oz Pernod
lemon peel

Pour gin and Pernod into an **aperitif glass**, fill with cold water, add lemon twist.

FRANZISKA (1984)

2 oz milk
³/₄ oz cream
³/₄ oz maracuja (passion fruit) juice
¹/₄ oz mango syrup
1 tablespoon honey

Heat and stir in a **heat-resistant glass** until honey is dissolved.

F

FRENCH COLADA (1982)

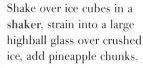

¾ oz cream
¾ oz coconut cream
1½ oz pineapple juice
¼ oz crème de cassis
¾ oz Cognac
1½ oz white rum
pineapple

Shake over ice cubes in a **shaker**, strain into a large highball glass over crushed ice, add pineapple chunks.

FRENCH DAIQUIRI

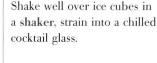

juice of half a lime
1 barspoon powdered sugar
dashes crème de cassis
2 oz white rum

Shake well over ice cubes in a **shaker**, strain into a chilled cocktail glass.

FRENCH 68 (1982)

¼ oz lemon juice
dash sugar syrup
dash grenadine
¾ oz Calvados
¼ oz brandy
Champagne

Shake first five ingredients well over ice cubes in a **shaker**, strain into a Champagne flute, slowly fill with Champagne.

F

FRENCH 75

$^1/_4$ oz lemon juice
dash sugar syrup
dash grenadine
$^3/_4$ oz gin
Champagne

Shake first four ingredients over ice cubes in a **shaker**, strain into a Champagne flute, fill with Champagne.

FRENCH 76

$^1/_4$ oz lemon juice
dash sugar syrup
dash grenadine
$^3/_4$ oz vodka
Champagne

Shake first four ingredients well over ice cubes in a **shaker**, strain into a Champagne flute, fill with Champagne.

FRIDAY

juice of a quarter lime
fruit from a quarter mango
$^3/_4$ oz mango syrup
$^3/_4$ oz white rum

Prepare in a **blender** with crushed ice, strain into a large highball glass, fill with crushed ice. Squeeze lime wedge over drink and drop it into the drink.

F

FRISCO SOUR

³/₄ oz lemon juice
1 barspoon powdered sugar
¹/₄ oz Bénédictine
1¹/₂ oz Bourbon
orange
stemmed cherry

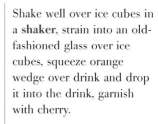

Shake well over ice cubes in a **shaker**, strain into an old-fashioned glass over ice cubes, squeeze orange wedge over drink and drop it into the drink, garnish with cherry.

FROZEN DAIQUIRI

³/₄ oz lime juice
2 barspoons powdered sugar
2 oz white rum

Prepare in a **blender** with crushed ice, pour into a cocktail glass.

FROZEN FRUIT DAIQUIRI*

³/₄ oz lime juice
fruit pieces (such as
    bananas)
1 barspoon powdered sugar
dashes of syrup of fruit
    used
2 oz white rum
dashes of dark rum

Prepare in a **blender** with crushed ice, pour into a cocktail glass.

*Well-known fruit daiquiris:
Banana Daiquiri
Pineapple Daiquiri
Strawberry Daiquiri*

FROZEN MARGARITA

³/₄ oz lemon juice
1 barspoon powdered sugar
³/₄ oz triple sec
1¹/₄ oz tequila

Prepare in a **blender** with crushed ice, pour into a cocktail glass.

FROZEN MATADOR

juice of half a lime
¹/₂ pineapple slice
1 barspoon powdered sugar
¹/₄ oz triple sec
1¹/₄ oz tequila

Prepare in a **blender** with crushed ice, pour into a small highball glass.

GAUGUIN (1986)

juice of half a lime
3/4 oz Rose's lime juice
fruit of a quarter cherimoya
1 1/2 oz white rum

Prepare in a **blender** with crushed ice, pour into a small highball glass, add squeezed lime half.

GENE TUNNEY

1/4 oz orange juice
dash lemon juice
3/4 oz dry vermouth
1 oz gin

Shake well over ice cubes in a **shaker**, strain into a chilled cocktail glass.

GIBSON

dash dry vermouth
2 oz gin
pearl onion

Stir in a **mixing glass** filled with ice, strain into a chilled martini glass, add pearl onion.

GIMLET*

2 oz gin
1³/₄ oz Rose's lime juice

Stir well over ice cubes in a **mixing glass**, strain into a chilled cocktail glass.

Original version Marlowe's Gin Gimlet

GIN & BITTERS*

dashes Angostura bitters
1¹/₄–1³/₄ oz gin

Rinse a **chilled sherry glass** with Angostura, pour in cold gin.

Pink Gin

GIN & IT

1¹/₂ oz gin
³/₄ oz vermouth rosso
orange

Stir over ice cubes in an **aperitif glass**, squeeze an orange wedge over drink and drop it into the drink.

G

GIN & SIN

3/4 oz lemon juice
1 barspoon powdered sugar
dashes grenadine
3/4 oz orange juice
1 1/2 oz gin

Shake well over ice cubes in a **shaker**, strain into a cocktail glass.

GIN FIZZ

1 oz lemon juice
1/4 oz sugar syrup
1 barspoon powdered sugar
2 oz gin
soda

Shake first four ingredients well over ice cubes in a **shaker**, strain into a collins glass filled with ice cubes, fill with soda.

GIN SOUR

3/4–1 oz lemon juice
1 barspoon powdered sugar
1/4 oz sugar syrup
1 1/2 oz gin
stemmed cherry

Shake well over ice cubes in a **shaker**, strain into a sour glass, add cherry.

G

GODFATHER

1 1/2 oz Bourbon
3/4 oz amaretto

Stir over ice in a **small high-ball glass**.

GODMOTHER

1 1/2 oz vodka
3/4 oz amaretto

Stir over ice in a **small high-ball glass**.

GOD'S CHILD

1 1/2 oz cream
1 barspoon powdered sugar
1/4 oz amaretto
1 oz vodka

Shake well over ice cubes in a **shaker**, strain into a cocktail glass.

GOLDEN CADILLAC

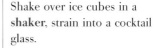

³/₄ oz cream
1 ¹/₂ oz orange juice
³/₄ oz crème de cacao
  (white)
¹/₄ oz Galliano

Shake over ice cubes in a
shaker, strain into a cocktail
glass.

GOLDEN COLADA (1983)

¹/₄ oz cream
³/₄ oz coconut cream
³/₄ oz pineapple juice
1 ¹/₂ oz orange juice
¹/₄ oz Galliano
³/₄ oz white rum
1 ¹/₂ oz dark rum
pineapple chunk
stemmed cherry

Shake over crushed ice in a
shaker, strain into a large
highball glass over crushed
ice, garnish with pineapple
chunk and cherry.

GOLDEN DREAM

³/₄ oz cream
1 ¹/₂ oz orange juice
³/₄ oz triple sec
¹/₄ oz Galliano

Shake over ice cubes in a
shaker, strain into a cocktail
glass.

GOLDEN FIZZ

1 oz lemon juice
1 egg yolk
1 barspoon powdered sugar
$^{1}/_{4}$ oz sugar syrup
$^{1}/_{4}$ oz orange juice
1 $^{1}/_{2}$ oz gin
soda

Shake first six ingredients well over ice cubes in a **shaker**, strain into a collins glass filled with ice cubes, carefully fill with soda.

GOLDEN NAIL

1 $^{1}/_{2}$ oz Bourbon
$^{3}/_{4}$ oz Southern Comfort

Stir over ice cubes in a **small highball glass**

GOLDEN RYE FIZZ

1 oz lemon juice
$^{1}/_{4}$ oz sugar syrup
$^{1}/_{4}$ oz egg liqueur (advocaat)
$^{1}/_{4}$ oz orange juice
1 $^{1}/_{2}$ oz rye whiskey
soda
cocktail cherry

Shake first five ingredients well over ice cubes in a **shaker**, strain into a collins glass over ice cubes, fill with soda, add cocktail cherry.

GOLDIE (1984)

$^1/_4$ oz cream
$1^1/_2$ oz milk
$^3/_4$ oz orange juice
1 barspoon powdered sugar
$1^1/_2$ oz dark rum
$^1/_4$ oz Galliano
orange peel

Heat in a **heat-resistant glass**, add orange peel.

GOOD MORNING EGGNOG (1990)*

1 egg yolk
1 barspoon powdered sugar
$1^3/_4$ oz ruby port
$1^3/_4$ oz Italian red wine
$3^1/_2$ oz milk
$^3/_4$ oz cream
nutmeg

Shake well over ice cubes in a **shaker**, strain into a large highball glass over ice cubes, sprinkle with nutmeg.

Schumann's version

GRASSHOPPER

$1^1/_2$ oz cream
$^3/_4$ oz crème de cacao
(white)
$^1/_4$ oz crème de menthe
(green)

Shake well over ice cubes in a **shaker**, strain into a sour glass.

GREEN DEVIL

³/₄ oz lemon juice
¹/₄ oz Rose's lime juice
1¹/₂ oz gin
¹/₄ oz crème de menthe
   (green)
soda

Shake first four ingredients
well over ice cubes in a
shaker, strain into a small
highball glass over ice cubes,
fill with soda.

GREEN LEAVES (1979)

mint leaves
³/₄ oz peppermint syrup
tonic water

Place mint leaves into a
large highball glass and
pour in peppermint syrup.
Press with a barspoon. Add a
scoop of crushed ice, fill
with tonic water, stir.

GREEN RUSSIAN*

1¹/₂ oz vodka
³/₄ oz crème de menthe
   (green)

Stir over crushed ice in a
small highball glass. (A
little soda can also be
added.)

Vodka Stinger

GREEN SPIDER

1 1/2 oz vodka
3/4 oz peppermint syrup
tonic water
mint sprig

Stir vodka and peppermint syrup well over ice cubes in a **collins glass**, fill with tonic water, garnish with mint sprig.

GREENBACK

1 1/2 oz gin
1/4 oz crème de menthe
   (green)
lime

Stir well over crushed ice in a **small highball glass**, squeeze lime wedge over drink and drop it into the drink.

GREYHOUND

2 oz vodka
grapefruit juice

Pour vodka over ice cubes in a **collins glass**, fill with grapefruit juice.

HABANA LIBRE

lime
dashes grenadine
1 1/2 oz white rum
3/4 oz white rum (extra
    aged)

Squeeze lime wedge into a
collins glass and drop into
the glass, add grenadine and
rum, fill with crushed ice,
stir well.

HAPPY NEW YEAR (1981)

1/4 oz brandy
3/4 oz ruby port
3/4 oz orange juice
Champagne

Shake first three ingredients
well over ice cubes in a
shaker, strain into a Champagne flute, fill with
Champagne.

HARVARD*

3/4 oz vermouth rosso
1 oz brandy
dash Angostura bitters

Stir in a **mixing glass** filled
with ice cubes, strain into a
chilled cocktail glass.

Brandy Manhattan

HARVEY WALLBANGER

1 1/2 oz vodka
3 1/2 oz orange juice
1/4 oz Galliano

Stir vodka and orange juice over ice cubes in a **collins glass**, add Galliano, and gently stir.

HAVANA SIDECAR

3/4 oz lemon juice
3/4 oz triple sec
1 1/2 oz gold rum

Shake well over ice cubes in a **shaker**, strain into a chilled cocktail glass.

HAVANA SPECIAL

2 oz pineapple juice
1/4 oz maraschino liqueur
1 1/2 oz white rum

Shake over crushed ice in a **shaker**, strain into a large highball glass over crushed ice.

HEMINGWAY*

3/4 oz Pernod
Champagne

Pour Pernod into a **Champagne flute**, fill with Champagne.

Corpse Reviver No. 2

HONOLULU JUICER

3/4 oz lemon juice
3/4 oz Rose's lime juice
1 barspoon powdered sugar
2 oz pineapple juice
1 1/2 oz Southern
    Comfort
3/4 oz dark rum
pineapple chunk

Shake well over ice cubes in a **shaker**, strain into a large highball glass over crushed ice, add pineapple.

HORSE'S NECK

2 oz Bourbon
dashes Angostura bitters
ginger ale
spiral lemon peel

Pour Bourbon over ice cubes in a **collins glass**, add Angostura, fill with ginger ale, drop spiral lemon peel into glass.

HOT BUTTERED RUM

1 sugar cube
2 oz dark rum
boiling water
butter

Crush sugar cube in a **heat-resistant glass** with a pestle, pour in rum, heat, fill with boiling water, grate ice-cold butter on top.

HOT FRENCHMAN (1982)

$^1/_8$ liter (4 oz) red wine
$^3/_4$ oz Grand Marnier
1 barspoon sugar
$^1/_4$ oz orange juice
$^1/_4$ oz lemon juice
lemon and orange
    peels

Heat well in a **heat-resistant glass**, stir, twist lemon and orange peels over drink and drop into the glass.

HOT JAMAICAN

juice of half a lime
$^1/_4$–$^3/_4$ oz sugar syrup
2 oz dark rum
boiling water
2 cloves
1 lime
$^1/_2$ cinnamon stick

Heat in a **heat-resistant glass**, fill with boiling water. Add lime slice pierced with cloves and cinnamon stick.

HOT M.M.M. (1983)

1 1/2 oz cream
1 1/2 oz milk
3/4 oz Tia Maria
1 oz dark rum
lemon and orange peel

Heat in a **heat-resistant glass**, twist lemon and orange peels over drink and drop into the glass.

HOT MARIE

3/4 oz brandy
3/4 oz dark rum
1/4 oz Tia Maria
1 cup hot coffee
sugar

Heat liquors in a **heat-resistant glass**, fill with hot coffee. (Add sugar to taste.)

HURRICANE

juice of half a lime
3/4 oz Rose's lime juice
1/4 oz maracuja (passion fruit) syrup
3/4 oz pineapple juice
3/4 oz orange juice
3/4 oz white rum
1 1/2 oz dark rum
lime

Shake over crushed ice in a **shaker**, strain into a large highball glass over crushed ice, add lime wedge.

I

I.B.F.*

dashes Fernet Branca
dashes triple sec
1 oz brandy
Champagne

Place an ice cube into a
Champagne flute, add
liquors, fill with Champagne.

International Bar Fly

I.B.U.

3/4 oz Cognac
3/4 oz orange juice
1/4 oz apricot brandy
Champagne

Shake over ice cubes in a
shaker, strain into a Champagne flute, fill with
Champagne.

ICED TEA (1990)*

juice of half a lime
3/4 oz orange juice
3/4 oz triple sec
3/4 oz brandy
3/4 oz dark rum
3/4–1 1/4 oz cola
1 cup cold tea

Stir well over crushed ice in
a **large highball glass**, add
squeezed lime half.

Schumann's version

IMPERIAL

1 oz dry vermouth
1 oz gin
dash maraschino liqueur
lemon peel

Stir well over ice cubes in a **mixing glass**, strain into a chilled martini glass, add a lemon twist.

INCOME TAX COCKTAIL

$3/4$ oz orange juice
$3/4$ oz dry vermouth
$3/4$ oz vermouth rosso
$3/4$ oz gin
dash Angostura bitters

Shake well over ice cubes in a **shaker**, strain into a chilled cocktail glass.

IRISH COFFEE

$1^1/2$ oz Irish whiskey
brown sugar
1 cup strong hot coffee
lightly whipped cream

Heat whiskey in a **heat-resistant glass** (do not boil), add sugar, fill with hot coffee, stir, top with cream.

ISLE OF PINES*

2 oz grapefruit juice
1 1/2 oz white rum

Stir over ice cubes in a **large highball glass**.

Isla de Pinos

ITALIAN COFFEE

1 oz Italian brandy
1/4 oz amaretto
1 cup hot espresso
brown sugar
cream

Heat brandy and amaretto in an **Irish coffee glass** (do not boil), add sugar, fill with hot espresso, stir, top with cream. (Galliano may be substituted for amaretto.)

ITALIAN COLADA (1986)

3/4 oz cream
1/4 oz coconut cream
2 oz pineapple juice
1/4 oz amaretto
3/4 oz white rum
3/4 oz Italian brandy
amarelle cherry

Shake well over ice cubes in a **shaker**, strain into a large highball glass over crushed ice, garnish with amarelle cherry. (Galliano may be substituted for amaretto.)

J

JACK ROSE

³/₄ oz lemon juice
1 barspoon powdered sugar
dashes grenadine
1¹/₂ oz Calvados

Shake over ice cubes in a **shaker**, strain into a chilled cocktail glass.

JADE

³/₄ oz lime juice
1 barspoon sugar
dash triple sec
dash crème de menthe
   (green)
1¹/₂ oz white rum

Shake well over ice cubes in a **shaker**, strain into a chilled cocktail glass.

JAMAICA FEVER (1982)

³/₄ oz lemon juice
³/₄ oz mango syrup
1¹/₂ oz pineapple juice
1¹/₂ oz dark rum
³/₄ oz brandy
pineapple chunk
stemmed cherry

Shake well over crushed ice in a **shaker**, pour into a large highball glass over crushed ice, add pineapple chunk and cherry.

J

JAMES BOND

1 sugar cube
dashes Angostura bitters
3/4–1 oz vodka
Champagne

Saturate sugar cube in a **Champagne flute** with Angostura, pour in vodka, fill with Champagne.

JEAN GABIN (1986)

1 1/2 oz dark rum
3/4 oz Calvados
1 tablespoon maple syrup
hot milk
nutmeg

Heat first three ingredients in a **heat-resistant glass**, fill with hot milk, sprinkle with nutmeg.

JEAN LAFITTE

1/4–3/4 oz lemon juice
1 egg yolk
1 barspoon powdered sugar
1/4 oz triple sec
1 1/2 oz gin
dash anisette

Shake over ice cubes in a **shaker**, strain into a cocktail glass.

J

JOGGING FLIP (1978)

various juices (such as
    lemon, orange, and grape-
    fruit juice)
1 egg yolk
dashes grenadine

Shake well over ice cubes in
a **shaker**, strain into a large
highball glass over crushed
ice.

JOURNALIST

¼ oz dry vermouth
¼ oz vermouth rosso
1 oz gin
dash lemon juice
dash triple sec
dash Angostura
    bitters

Stir over ice cubes in a
mixing glass, strain into a
chilled cocktail glass.

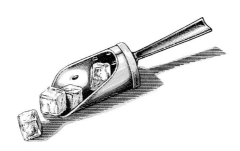

K

KAMIKAZE

¼ oz lemon juice
¾ oz Rose's lime juice
dash triple sec
1½ oz vodka

Shake well over ice cubes in a **shaker**, strain into a chilled cocktail glass.

KIR

1 barspoon crème de cassis
dry white wine

Spoon cassis into a **wine glass**, fill with white wine.

KIR ROYAL

1 barspoon crème de cassis
Champagne

Spoon cassis into a **Champagne flute**, fill with Champagne.

K

KNICKERBOCKER COCKTAIL

³/₄ oz dry vermouth
dashes vermouth bianco
   (or vermouth rosso)
1 oz gin
lemon peel

Stir well in a **mixing glass** filled with ice cubes, strain into a chilled martini glass, squeeze lemon twist over drink and drop into the glass.

KNOCKOUT COCKTAIL

³/₄ oz dry vermouth
³/₄ oz gin
dashes Pernod
dash crème de menthe
   (white)

Stir over ice cubes in a **mixing glass**, strain into a chilled martini glass.

LA FLORIDITA COCKTAIL

juice of half a lime
dash grenadine
dashes crème de cacao
    (white)
$3/4$ oz vermouth rosso
$1^1/_2$ oz white rum

Shake well over ice cubes in a **shaker**, strain into a chilled cocktail glass.

LA FLORIDITA DAIQUIRI

juice of a lime
1 barspoon powdered sugar
    (or sugar syrup)
$1/_4$ oz maraschino liqueur
2 oz white rum

Shake well over crushed ice in a **shaker**, strain into a chilled cocktail glass.

LADIES SIDECAR (1984)

$^1/_4$ oz lemon juice
$^1/_4$ oz triple sec
1 oz orange juice
1 oz brandy

Shake well over ice cubes in
a **shaker**, strain into a chilled
cocktail glass.

LATE MISTRAL (1980)

1$^1/_2$ oz vodka
$^1/_4$ oz Ricard
lemon peel

Pour into an **aperitif glass**
over ice cubes, fill with cold
water, stir, add lemon peel.

LATIN LOVER (1984)

$^1/_4$–$^3/_4$ oz lemon juice
$^3/_4$ oz Rose's lime juice
1$^1/_4$–2 oz pineapple juice
$^3/_4$ oz cachaça
$^3/_4$ oz tequila
pineapple

Shake well over crushed ice
in a **shaker**, strain into a
large highball glass over
crushed ice, add pineapple.

L

LEAP YEAR*

3/4 oz vermouth rosso
1/4 oz Grand Marnier
1 oz gin
dashes lemon juice

Shake well over ice cubes in a **shaker**, strain into a chilled cocktail glass.

Harry Craddock, Feb. 29, 1928, Savoy Hotel, London

LEAVE IT TO ME

dashes lemon juice
dashes maraschino liqueur
3/4 oz dry vermouth
3/4 oz gin
dashes apricot
    brandy

Shake over ice cubes in a **shaker**, strain into a martini glass.

LEMON SQUASH

lemon or lime
2–3 barspoons sugar

Place a peeled and quartered lemon into a **large highball glass**, add sugar, press with a pestle, fill with water, and stir again.

L

LEMONADE

1 ½ oz lemon juice
sugar syrup
  (or sugar)
soda

Stir lemon juice and sugar well in a **large highball glass**, add ice cubes, fill with soda, and stir again.

LEMONADE GOLDEN

1 ½ oz lemon juice
1 egg yolk
sugar syrup
  (or sugar)
soda

Shake first three ingredients well over ice cubes in a **shaker**, strain into a large highball glass over ice cubes, carefully fill with water or soda.

Harry Craddock, famous bartender of the Savoy Hotel bar, London, was once asked, "What is the best way to drink a cocktail?"

"Quickly," replied that great man, "while it's still laughing at you."

LIBERTY COCKTAIL

lime
1 sugar cube
3/4 oz Calvados
3/4 oz white rum
(or dark)

Press sugar cube on a lime wedge in a **small highball glass**, pour in liquors, stir well, add ice cubes, stir again.

LOFTUS SPECIAL (1986)

juice of 1 1/2 limes
dashes grenadine
1/4 oz sugar syrup
3/4 oz Cherry Heering
3/4 oz apricot brandy
3/4 oz white rum
1 1/2 oz dark rum
1 1/2 oz high-proof
dark rum

Shake well over crushed ice in a **shaker**, strain into a large highball glass over crushed ice, add squeezed lime wedge.

LONE TREE

3/4 oz dry vermouth
1/4 oz vermouth rosso
dash orange bitters
3/4 oz gin

Stir well over ice cubes in a **mixing glass**, strain into a chilled martini glass.

LONG DISTANCE RUNNER (1986)

pineapple slice
juice of half a lime
2 oz pineapple juice
¹/₄ oz maracuja (passion
    fruit) syrup

Prepare in a blender with
crushed ice, strain into a
large highball glass, fill with
crushed ice.

LONG ISLAND ICED TEA*

¹/₂ lime
³/₄ oz orange juice
¹/₄ oz triple sec
³/₄ oz white rum
³/₄ oz gin
³/₄ oz vodka
cola

Squeeze lime into a **collins
glass**, add ice cubes, pour in
liquors and juice, stir well,
fill with cola.

original version

*I personally never pour vodka
and gin together.*

MACARONI

$^3/_4$ oz vermouth bianco
dash Pernod

Stir over ice cubes in an **aperitif glass**, fill with water, and stir.

MAI TAI

juice of a lime
$1^1/_2$ oz Rose's lime juice
dash orgeat syrup
$^1/_4$ oz apricot brandy
1 barspoon powdered sugar
2 oz dark rum
$^3/_4$ oz high-proof dark rum
lime, mint

Shake well over crushed ice in a **shaker**, pour into a large highball glass over crushed ice, add squeezed lime wedge, garnish with mint sprig.

MALCOLM LOWRY (1984)

$^3/_4$ oz lemon juice
$^1/_4$–$^3/_4$ oz triple sec
$^1/_4$ oz white rum
1 oz tequila

Shake well over ice cubes in a **shaker**, strain into a chilled cocktail glass. (Cocktail glass may be rimmed with salt.)

MANDEVILLE

dash lemon juice
dash grenadine
dash anisette
³/₄ oz white rum
³/₄ oz dark rum
cola

Stir first five ingredients well over ice cubes in a **large highball glass**, fill with cola.

MANHATTAN DRY

1¹/₂ oz Canadian whisky
³/₄ oz dry vermouth
dashes Angostura bitters
lemon peel

Stir well in a **mixing glass** filled with ice cubes, strain into a chilled cocktail glass, add lemon twist.

MANHATTAN PERFECT

1¹/₂ oz Canadian whisky
¹/₄ oz dry vermouth
¹/₄ oz vermouth rosso
dashes Angostura bitters
stemmed cherry

Stir well in a **mixing glass** filled with ice cubes, strain into a chilled cocktail glass, garnish with cherry.

MANHATTAN SWEET

1 1/2 oz Canadian whisky
3/4 oz vermouth rosso
dashes Angostura bitters
stemmed cherry

Stir well in a **mixing glass** filled with ice cubes, strain into a chilled cocktail glass, garnish with cherry.

MARADONA (1986)

1 1/2 oz milk
3 1/2 oz maracuja (passion
    fruit) juice
3/4 oz maracuja syrup

Shake well over ice cubes in a **shaker**, strain into a large highball glass over crushed ice.

MARGARITA

3/4 oz lemon juice
3/4 oz Cointreau
    (or triple sec)
1 1/2 oz tequila

Shake well over ice cubes in a **shaker**, strain into a chilled cocktail glass with a salted rim.

MARTINEZ COCKTAIL

³/₄ oz dry vermouth
dash orange bitters
dash triple sec
1¹/₂ oz gin
lemon peel

Stir well in a **mixing glass** filled with ice cubes, strain into a chilled martini glass, twist lemon peel over drink and drop into the glass.

MARTIN'S RUM-ORANGE PUNCH (1982)

³/₄ oz lemon juice
³/₄ oz Rose's lime juice
1 barspoon powdered sugar
dashes sugar syrup
1¹/₂ oz orange juice
¹/₄ oz Southern Comfort
1¹/₄ oz dark rum
¹/₄ oz high-proof dark rum
lemon and orange peels

Heat well in a **heat-resistant glass**, twist lemon and orange peels over drink and drop into glass.

MARTINI

¹/₂ teaspoon dry vermouth
  (or to taste)
1¹/₂ oz gin
1 green olive with pit

Stir in a **mixing glass** filled with ice cubes, strain into a chilled martini glass, add olive.

MARY PICKFORD

1½ oz pineapple juice
dash grenadine
dash maraschino liqueur
1½ oz white rum
lime peel

Shake over ice cubes in a **shaker**, strain into a chilled cocktail glass, twist lime peel over drink and drop into the glass.

MAURICE CHEVALIER

¾ oz vermouth rosso
¾ oz Noilly Prat French dry
   vermouth
dash orange bitters
¾ oz orange juice
¾ oz gin

Shake well over ice cubes in a **shaker**, strain into a chilled cocktail glass.

MERRY WIDOW NO. 1

¾ oz dry vermouth
dash Bénédictine
dash orange bitters
dash anisette
¾ oz gin
lemon peel

Stir well in a **mixing glass** filled with ice cubes, strain into a chilled cocktail glass, twist lemon peel over drink and drop into the glass.

MERRY WIDOW NO. 2

¾ oz dry vermouth
¾ oz Dubonnet
¾ oz vodka
dash orange bitters
lemon peel

Stir well in a **mixing glass** filled with ice cubes, strain into a chilled cocktail glass, twist lemon peel over drink and drop into the glass.

MEXICAN COFFEE (1982)

1½ oz gold tequila
¼ oz Kahlúa
1 barspoon brown sugar
1 cup strong hot coffee
lightly whipped cream

Heat liquors in a **heat-resistant glass** (do not boil). Add sugar and allow to dissolve, fill with coffee and stir well, top with cream.

MEXICAN COLADA (1986)

¾ oz cream
¼ oz coconut cream
2 oz pineapple juice
¼ oz Kahlúa
1½ oz tequila

Shake over crushed ice in a **shaker**, strain into a large highball glass over crushed ice.

M

MEXICANA

¹/₄ oz lemon juice
dash grenadine
1 ¹/₂ oz pineapple juice
1 ¹/₂ oz tequila

Shake well over crushed ice
in a **shaker**, strain into a
small highball glass half-
filled with crushed ice.

MILLIONAIRE

³/₄ oz lemon juice
1 egg white
¹/₄ oz triple sec
dashes grenadine
1 ¹/₂ oz Bourbon

Shake well over ice cubes in
a **shaker**, strain into a sour
glass.

MIMOSA

1 ¹/₂ oz orange juice (fresh)
Champagne

Pour orange juice into
Champagne flute, carefully
fill glass with Champagne.

MINT DAIQUIRI

a few mint leaves
juice of half a lime
1 barspoon powdered sugar
¹/₄ oz Cointreau
2 oz white rum

Prepare in a **blender** with crushed ice, strain into a cocktail glass.

MINT JULEP (GEORGIA STYLE)*

mint leaves and sprigs
2 sugar cubes
¹/₄ oz peach brandy
1¹/₂ oz brandy

Crush mint leaves and sugar cubes in a **large highball glass** with a pestle. Fill with crushed ice, pour in liquors, stir well, garnish with mint sprig.

*MINT JULEPS USING THE FOLLOWING LIQUORS ARE FAMOUS:

Bourbon whiskey
Champagne
white or dark rum
brandy

Mint Julep "Southern Style"
Champagne Julep
Rum Julep
Brandy Julep

MOJITO

juice of half a lime
1 barspoon powdered sugar
2 oz white rum
soda
mint sprig

Stir sugar and lime juice well in a **large highball glass**. Crush mint leaves with a pestle, add the squeezed half lime. Fill with crushed ice, add rum, stir. Add soda, garnish with mint sprig.

MONKEY GLAND

1 oz orange juice
dash grenadine
dash Pernod
1 oz gin

Shake well over ice cubes in a **shaker**, strain into a chilled cocktail glass.

MONTE CARLO IMPERIAL

$1/4$–$3/4$ oz lemon juice
$1/4$ oz crème de menthe
    (white)
$3/4$ oz gin
Champagne

Shake first three ingredients well over ice cubes in a **shaker**, strain into a Champagne flute, fill with Champagne.

MORNING GLORY FIZZ

³/₄–1 oz lemon juice
¹/₄–³/₄ oz sugar syrup
1 egg white
1 barspoon powdered sugar
dash Pernod
1 ¹/₂ oz Scotch
soda

Shake first six ingredients well over ice cubes in a **shaker**, strain into a collins glass over ice cubes, fill with soda.

MOSCOW MULE

1 ¹/₂ oz vodka
ginger beer (or ginger ale)
spiral lemon peel

Pour vodka over ice cubes in a **collins glass**, fill with ginger beer, stir, add spiral lemon peel.

MUDDY RIVER*

1 ¹/₂ oz Kahlúa
1 ¹/₂ oz cream

Stir over ice cubes in a **small highball glass**

Kahlúa Cream

MULATA

juice of half a lime
¹/₄ oz crème de cacao
(brown)
¹/₄ oz sugar syrup
2 oz white rum

Prepare in a **blender** with crushed ice, strain into a cocktail glass.

NEGRONI

3/4 oz vermouth rosso
3/4 oz Campari
1/4–3/4 oz gin
lemon peel

Stir over ice cubes in an **aperitif glass**, twist lemon peel over drink and drop into glass.

NEW ORLEANS FIZZ*

1 oz lemon juice
1 egg white
1 barspoon powdered sugar
1/4–3/4 oz sugar syrup
dash fleurs d'orange (orange flower water)
1/4 oz cream
2 oz gin
soda

Shake first seven ingredients well over ice cubes in a **shaker**, strain into a collins glass filled with ice cubes, fill with soda.

*Ramos Fizz

NEW ORLEANS SAZERAC

1 sugar cube
dash Angostura bitters
2 oz Bourbon
1/4 oz Pernod
lemon peel

Place sugar cube in an **old-fashioned glass**, saturate with Angostura, add ice cubes, pour in liquors, twist lemon peel over drink, fill with water, stir well.

NEW YORK FLIP

1 egg yolk
1/4 oz sugar syrup
3/4 oz cream
1 oz Bourbon
3/4 oz tawny port
nutmeg

Shake well over ice cubes in a **shaker**, strain into a cocktail glass. Sprinkle with nutmeg.

NEW YORKER

1 1/2 oz Bourbon
lime
dashes grenadine

Pour Bourbon over ice cubes in an **old-fashioned glass**, squeeze lime wedge into drink and drop into glass, add grenadine, stir well.

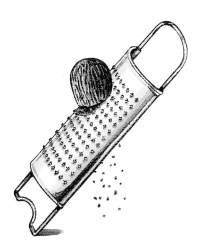

OHIO

$3/4$ oz vermouth rosso
$3/4$ oz Canadian whisky
dash triple sec
dash Angostura bitters
Champagne

Stir first four ingredients in a **mixing glass** filled with ice cubes, strain into a Champagne flute, fill with Champagne.

OLD-FASHIONED

1 sugar cube
dashes Angostura bitters
2 oz Bourbon
soda
stemmed cherry
orange
lemon

Place sugar cube in an **old-fashioned glass**, saturate with Angostura, add orange and lemon wedges, press with a pestle, add Bourbon, stir well, add ice cubes, fill with soda or water, stir again, garnish with cherry.

OLYMPIC

$3/4$ oz orange juice
$1/4$ oz triple sec
$1 1/2$ oz brandy
dash lemon juice

Shake well over ice cubes in a **shaker**, strain into a chilled cocktail glass.

OPAL

³/₄ oz dry vermouth
³/₄ oz gin
dashes Pernod

Stir well over ice cubes in a **mixing glass**, strain into a chilled cocktail glass.

OPERA

³/₄ oz Dubonnet
³/₄ oz gin
dash maraschino liqueur
lemon peel

Stir over ice cubes in a **small highball glass**, twist lemon peel over drink and drop into glass.

ORANGE BLOSSOM

1³/₄ oz gin
1³/₄ oz orange juice
dashes fleurs d'orange
   (orange flower water)

Shake well over ice cubes in a **shaker**, strain into a chilled cocktail glass.

ORANGEADE

juice of 2 oranges
sugar syrup
orange
lemon

Pour orange juice into a **small highball glass**, fill with water, and sweeten to taste. Squeeze orange and lemon wedges over drink, drop into glass, and stir.

ORDINARY SEAMAN

$3/4$ oz lemon juice
$3/4$ oz Rose's lime juice
1 barspoon powdered sugar
1 oz dark rum
$3/4$ oz white rum
lime

Shake well over crushed ice in a **shaker**, strain into a small highball glass over crushed ice, squeeze lime wedge into drink and drop it into the glass.

PALMER

dash lemon juice
dash Angostura bitters
1³/₄ oz Bourbon
lemon

Pour Bourbon over ice cubes
in an **old-fashioned glass**,
add a dash of Angostura,
squeeze lemon wedge over
drink and drop into glass,
stir well.

PARADISE

1¹/₄ oz orange juice
¹/₄ oz apricot brandy
1¹/₂ oz gin

Shake well over ice cubes in
a **shaker**, strain into a cocktail glass.

PARISIENNE

³/₄ oz Noilly Prat
³/₄ oz gin
dashes crème de cassis

Stir well over ice cubes in a
mixing glass, strain into a
chilled cocktail glass over an
ice cube.

P

PARK AVENUE

¹/₄ oz dry vermouth
¹/₄ oz vermouth bianco
1 oz gin
¹/₄ oz pineapple juice
    (unsweetened)

Stir well on ice cubes in a **mixing glass**, strain into a chilled cocktail glass.

PARK LANE

¹/₄ oz lemon juice
dash grenadine
1¹/₂ oz orange juice
¹/₄ oz apricot brandy
1¹/₂ oz gin

Shake well over ice cubes in a **shaker**, strain into a chilled cocktail glass.

PEACH DAIQUIRI

piece of peach
juice of a quarter lime
1 barspoon powdered sugar
2 oz white rum
¹/₄ oz peach brandy

Prepare in a **blender** with crushed ice, pour into a cocktail glass.

P

PELICAN (1986)

dash lemon juice
dash grenadine
$^1/_4$ oz lime syrup
$3^1/_2$ oz grapefruit juice

Shake well over ice cubes in a **shaker**, strain into a large highball glass over ice cubes.

PEPE (1984)

$^1/_4$ oz lemon juice
$^1/_4$ oz Rose's lime juice
dash triple sec
2 oz grapefruit juice
1 oz tequila
$^3/_4$ oz cachaça

Shake well over ice cubes in a **shaker**, strain into a large highball glass over crushed ice.

PEPINOS CAFÉ (1982)

1 oz tequila
$^1/_4$–$^3/_4$ oz Kahlúa
1 barspoon brown sugar
1 cup strong hot coffee
lightly whipped cream

Heat tequila and Kahlúa in a **heat-resistant glass**, stir in sugar, fill with coffee, stir again, top with cream.

PERFECT COCKTAIL

³/₄ oz dry vermouth
³/₄ oz vermouth rosso
³/₄ oz gin
orange peel

Stir well over ice cubes in a **mixing glass**, strain into a chilled cocktail glass, twist orange peel over drink and drop into glass.

PERIODISTA

juice of half a lime
1 barspoon powdered sugar
¹/₄ oz apricot brandy
¹/₄ oz triple sec
1¹/₂ oz white rum
lime peel

Shake well over ice cubes in a **shaker**, strain into a cocktail glass, twist lime peel over drink and drop into glass.

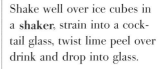

PERROQUET

1¹/₂ oz Pernod
dashes peppermint syrup

Pour over ice cubes in an **aperitif glass**, fill with cold water, and stir well.

PICASSO

dash lemon juice
3/4 oz Dubonnet
1 oz brandy
lemon
orange

Stir over ice cubes in a **small highball glass**, twist lemon and orange peels over drink and drop into glass.

PICK-ME-UP

1/4 oz lemon juice
dash Angostura bitters
dash sugar syrup
dash grenadine
3/4–1 oz brandy
Champagne

Shake first five ingredients well over ice cubes in a **shaker**, strain into a Champagne flute, fill with Champagne.

PIMM'S NO. 1

1 1/4 –1 3/4 oz Pimm's No. 1
Seven-Up
lemon peel
cucumber peel

Pour Pimm's over ice cubes in a **large highball glass**, fill with Seven-Up, add lemon and cucumber peels.

PIMM'S RANGOON

1 1/4–1 3/4 oz Pimm's No. 1
ginger ale
lemon peel
cucumber peel

Prepare same as Pimm's
No. 1.

PIMM'S ROYAL

1 1/4–1 3/4 oz Pimm's No. 1
Champagne
lemon peel
cucumber peel

Prepare same as Pimm's
No. 1.

PIÑA COLADA*

1 1/4 oz coconut cream
2 oz pineapple juice
2 oz white rum

Prepare in a **blender** with
crushed ice, pour into a large
highball glass.

original version

PIÑA COLADA (SCHUMANN'S)

$^3/_4$ oz sweet cream
$^3/_4$ oz coconut cream
2 oz pineapple juice
1$^1/_4$ oz dark rum
$^3/_4$ oz white rum
pineapple chunk
amarelle cherry

Prepare in a **shaker** over crushed ice, strain into a large highball glass over crushed ice. Garnish with pineapple chunk and amarelle cherry.

PINEAPPLE DAIQUIRI

pineapple slice
dashes pineapple syrup
juice of a quarter lime
1 barspoon powdered sugar
2 oz white rum

Prepare in a **blender** with crushed ice, pour into a chilled cocktail glass.

PINERITO

juice of half a lime
dash grenadine
2 barspoons powdered sugar
2$^3/_4$ oz grapefruit juice
2 oz white rum

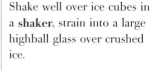

Shake well over ice cubes in a **shaker**, strain into a large highball glass over crushed ice.

PINK CREOLE

dashes lemon juice
dash grenadine
$^1/_4$ oz cream
2 oz white rum

Shake well over ice cubes in a **shaker**, strain into a cocktail glass.

PINK DAIQUIRI

juice of half a lime
2 barspoons powdered sugar
dashes grenadine
2 oz white rum

Shake well over ice cubes in a **shaker**, strain into a chilled cocktail glass.

PINK GIN*

dashes Angostura bitters
1$^3/_4$ oz gin

Rinse a **chilled sherry glass** with Angostura, pour in gin. (Ice water can be added if desired.)

*Gin & Bitters

P

PINK LADY

¹/₄ oz lemon juice
1 egg white
1 barspoon powdered sugar
dashes grenadine
1¹/₂ oz gin

Shake well over ice cubes in a **shaker**, strain into a sour glass.

PINKY COLADA

³/₄ oz pineapple juice
³/₄ oz cream
1¹/₄ oz milk
³/₄ oz coconut cream
dashes grenadine
2 oz white rum
amarelle cherry

Shake well over ice cubes in a **shaker**, strain into a large highball glass over crushed ice, garnish with amarelle cherry.

PIPELINE

³/₄ oz lemon juice
¹/₄ oz apricot brandy
1 barspoon powdered sugar
1¹/₂ oz Bacardi

Shake well over ice cubes in a **shaker**, strain into a chilled cocktail glass.

PISCO SOUR

³/₄ oz lemon juice
¹/₄ oz sugar syrup
1 ¹/₂ oz Pisco brandy
stemmed cherry

Shake well over ice cubes in a **shaker**, strain into a sour glass, garnish with cherry.

PLANTER'S PUNCH

³/₄ oz lemon juice
¹/₄ oz grenadine
2³/₄ oz orange juice
1³/₄–2 oz dark rum
orange
stemmed cherry
nutmeg

Shake well over ice cubes in a shaker, strain into a **large highball glass** over ice cubes, add orange wedge and cherry, sprinkle with nutmeg.

POLAR BEAR

1 ¹/₂ oz cream
³/₄ oz crème de cacao
(white)
1 ¹/₂ oz vodka

Shake well over ice cubes in a **shaker**, strain into a cocktail glass.

P

PORTO FLIP

1 egg yolk
1 barspoon powdered sugar
3/4 oz cream
1 1/2 oz ruby port
1/4 oz brandy
nutmeg

Shake well over ice cubes in a **shaker**, strain into a cocktail glass, sprinkle with nutmeg.

PRAIRIE OYSTER

olive oil
1–2 tablespoons tomato
    ketchup
1 egg yolk
salt, pepper
Tabasco
Worcestershire sauce
vinegar or lemon juice

Rinse a **cocktail glass** with olive oil, place ketchup in glass, carefully add egg yolk, and season. (Serve with a small spoon and a glass of ice water.)

PRESIDENTE*

1/4 oz dry vermouth
3/4 oz vermouth rosso
1 1/2 oz white rum
dash grenadine
stemmed cherry

Stir over ice cubes in a **mixing glass**, strain into a chilled cocktail glass, garnish with cherry.

*original version

PRINCE OF WALES

1 sugar cube
dashes Angostura bitters
³/₄ oz Cognac
orange
stemmed cherry
Champagne
¹/₄ oz Bénédictine

Place sugar cube into a
small highball glass
(originally a silver glass),
saturate with Angostura, add
ice cube, pour in cognac,
add orange wedge and
cherry, fill with
Champagne,
gradually pour
in Bénédictine.

PRINCETON

³/₄ oz white port
1 oz brandy
dash orange bitters

Stir well in a **mixing glass**
filled with ice cubes, strain
into a chilled cocktail glass.

PUNCH À LA
WASHINGTON HOTEL (1986)

juice of half a lime
passion fruit (or 2³/₄ oz
    maracuja juice)
¹/₄ oz maracuja (passion
    fruit) syrup
1 oz white rum
1 oz dark rum

Prepare in a **blender** if fruit
is used; otherwise shake well
over ice cubes in a **shaker**
and strain into a large highball glass over crushed ice.

PUSSY FOOT

¹/₄ oz lemon juice
dash grenadine
1³/₄ oz orange juice
1³/₄ oz grapefruit juice
stemmed cherry

Shake well over ice cubes in
a **shaker**, strain into a small
highball glass over ice cubes,
garnish with cherry.

Q

QUAKER'S

$^3/_4$ oz lemon juice
1 barspoon powdered sugar
dash cranberry syrup
$^3/_4$ oz brandy
$^3/_4$ oz white rum

Shake well over ice cubes in a **shaker**, strain into a chilled cocktail glass.

QUARTER DECK

$^1/_2$ lime
$^3/_4$ oz cream sherry
1 oz white rum

Squeeze lime over ice cubes in a **small highball glass** and drop into glass, pour in sherry and rum, stir well.

R

RATTLESNAKE

³/₄ oz lemon juice
1 egg white
1 barspoon powdered sugar
¹/₄ oz sugar syrup
1¹/₂ oz Bourbon
dash anisette

Shake well over ice cubes in a **shaker**, strain into a cocktail glass.

RED LION

1¹/₂ oz orange juice
¹/₄ oz lemon juice
dash grenadine
³/₄ oz Grand Marnier
1 oz gin

Shake well over ice cubes in a **shaker**, strain into a cocktail glass.

RED MOUTH (1984)

1¹/₄ oz milk
³/₄ oz cream
³/₄ oz Cherry Heering
³/₄ oz white rum

Heat in a **heat-resistant glass**.

R

RED RUSSIAN (1990)

1 ½ oz vodka
¾ oz Cherry Heering

Stir over ice cubes in a mixing glass, strain into an **aperitif glass**.

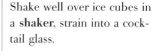

RED SNAPPER

2 oz cream
dash grenadine
¼ oz Galliano
1 oz white rum

Shake well over ice cubes in a **shaker**, strain into a cocktail glass.

RITZ

¾ oz orange juice
¾ oz Cognac
¼ oz Cointreau
Champagne

Shake first three ingredients over ice cubes in a **shaker**, strain into a Champagne flute, carefully fill with Champagne.

R

ROBINSON (1986)

juice of a quarter lime
papaya fruit
$^1/_4$–$^3/_4$ oz sugar syrup
1 oz white rum
1 oz dark rum

Prepare in a **blender** with crushed ice, pour into a large highball glass.

ROB ROY*

$^1/_2$ oz dry vermouth
$^1/_2$ oz vermouth rosso
1 oz Scotch
dash Angostura bitters
stemmed cherry

Stir in a **mixing glass** filled with ice cubes, strain into a chilled cocktail glass, garnish with cherry.

Perfect, Scotch Manhattan

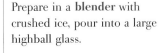

ROLLS-ROYCE

$^3/_4$ oz dry vermouth
$^3/_4$ oz vermouth rosso
$^3/_4$ oz gin
dash Bénédictine
stemmed cherry

Stir in a **mixing glass** filled with ice cubes, strain into a chilled cocktail glass, garnish with cherry.

RORY O'MORE*

¾ oz vermouth rosso
1½ oz Irish whiskey
dash orange bitters

Stir in a **mixing glass** filled with ice, strain into a chilled cocktail glass.

Irish Manhattan

ROSE—ENGLISH

¼ oz lemon juice
dash apricot brandy
dash grenadine
¾ oz dry vermouth
¾ oz gin

Stir well in a **mixing glass** filled with ice cubes, strain into a chilled cocktail glass.

ROSE—FRENCH

¾ oz dry vermouth
¼ oz eau-de-vie de cerises
   (kirschwasser)
¾ oz gin
dash grenadine

Stir in a **mixing glass** filled with ice cubes, strain into a chilled cocktail glass.

R

ROSITA

$^1/_4$ oz dry vermouth
$^1/_4$ oz vermouth rosso
$^1/_4$ oz Campari
$^3/_4$ oz tequila

Stir over ice cubes in a
mixing glass, strain into a
chilled cocktail glass.

ROYAL GIN FIZZ

1 oz lemon juice
1 egg
1 barspoon powdered sugar
$^1/_4$ oz sugar syrup
2 oz gin
Champagne

Shake first five ingredients
very vigorously over ice
cubes in a **shaker**, strain into
a collins glass over ice cubes,
fill with Champagne.

RUBY FIZZ

$^3/_4$ oz lemon juice
1 egg white
1 barspoon powdered sugar
$^1/_4$ oz sugar syrup
$^3/_4$ oz gin
$^3/_4$ oz sloe gin
soda

Shake first six ingredients
very vigorously over ice
cubes in a **shaker**, strain into
a collins glass over ice cubes,
fill with soda.

RUM ALEXANDER

1 oz cream
3/4 oz crème de cacao
    (brown)
1 1/2 oz white rum
nutmeg

Shake well over ice cubes in
a **shaker**, strain into a cocktail glass, sprinkle with
nutmeg.

RUM EGGNOG

1 egg white
1/4 oz sugar syrup
1 barspoon powdered sugar
3 1/2 oz milk
3/4 oz cream
3/4 oz white rum
3/4 oz dark rum
nutmeg

Shake well over ice cubes in
a **shaker**, strain into a large
highball glass over ice cubes,
sprinkle with nutmeg.

RUM FIZZ

3/4 oz lemon juice
1/4–3/4 oz sugar syrup
2 oz white rum
soda

Shake well over ice in a
shaker, strain into a collins
glass over ice cubes, fill with
soda.

RUM GIMLET

³/₄ oz lemon juice
1 oz Rose's lime juice
2 oz white rum

Shake over ice cubes in a
shaker, strain into a chilled
cocktail glass.

RUM HIGHBALL

2 oz white rum (or dark)
ginger ale, soda, or
    Seven-Up
spiral lemon peel

Pour rum over ice cubes into
a **collins glass**, fill with
ginger ale, add spiral lemon
peel.

RUM OLD FASHIONED

1 sugar cube
dashes Angostura bitters
lemon, orange
2 oz white rum
water or soda

Place sugar cube in an **old-
fashioned glass** and saturate
with Angostura, add lemon
and orange wedges, and
crush with pestle. Add ice
cubes, pour in rum, stir, fill
with soda.

RUM RUNNER (1986)

juice of half a lime
1 barspoon powdered sugar
  (or ¼ oz sugar syrup)
2¾ oz pineapple juice
1 oz white rum
1 oz dark rum
dash Angostura bitters
nutmeg

Shake over crushed ice in a
shaker, strain into a large
highball glass, fill with
crushed ice, sprinkle with
nutmeg.

RUM SAZERAC

1 sugar cube
dashes Angostura bitters
2 oz white rum
dashes Pernod

Crush Angostura-soaked
sugar cube with a pestle in
an **old-fashioned glass**, add
ice cubes, pour in rum, add
dashes of Pernod, fill with
water.

RUM SCREWDRIVER

3¹/₂ oz orange juice
2 oz white rum

Stir over ice cubes in a **collins glass**.

RUM SOUR

³/₄ oz lemon juice
¹/₄–³/₄ oz sugar syrup
dashes dark rum
1¹/₂ oz white rum
stemmed cherry

Shake well over ice cubes in a **shaker**, strain into a sour glass, garnish with cherry.

RUM STINGER

³/₄ oz crème de menthe
   (white)
1¹/₂ oz white rum

Stir over ice in a **small highball glass**.

RUSSIAN BEAR

1 ½ oz cream
1 oz vodka
¼ oz crème de cacao
   (brown)
1 barspoon powdered
   sugar

Shake over ice cubes in a
shaker, strain into a cocktail
glass.

RUSSIAN CADILLAC

1 oz cream
1 oz vodka
¾ oz Galliano
¼ oz crème de cacao
   (white)

Shake over ice cubes in a
shaker, strain into a cocktail
glass.

RUSTY NAIL

1 ½ oz Scotch
¾ oz Drambuie

Stir over ice cubes in a **small
highball glass**.

RYE SLING

1 oz lemon juice
¼ oz sugar syrup
1½ oz rye whiskey
¼ oz Cherry Heering
soda
cocktail cherry

Shake first four ingredients well over ice cubes in a **shaker**, strain into a collins glass over ice cubes, fill with soda, garnish with cocktail cherry.

RYE SOUR

1 oz lemon juice
¼–¾ oz sugar syrup (or 1 barspoon sugar)
1½ oz rye whiskey
stemmed cherry

Shake well over ice cubes in a **shaker**, strain into a sour glass, add cherry.

S

SALTY DOG

2 oz vodka
2 oz grapefruit juice

Shake over ice cubes in a **shaker**, strain into a chilled cocktail glass rimmed with salt.

SAOCO

3 1/2 oz coconut milk
1 1/2 oz white rum

Stir over crushed ice in a **collins glass**.

SAZERAC*

1 sugar cube
dashes Angostura bitters (or Peychaud bitters)
1 1/2 oz rye whiskey
1/4 oz Pernod
water or soda

Place Angostura-saturated sugar cube into an **old-fashioned glass**, crush with a barspoon, add liquors, mix well, fill with water.

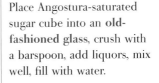

original version

SCHUMANN'S GIMLET (1983)

¾ oz lemon juice
1¼ oz Rose's lime juice
2 oz gin

Shake well over ice cubes in a **shaker**, strain into a chilled cocktail glass.

SCOFFLAW

¼ oz lemon juice
dash grenadine
1 oz dry vermouth
1 oz Canadian whisky
dash orange bitters

Stir well over ice cubes in a **mixing glass**, strain into a chilled cocktail glass.

SCORPION

juice of half a lime
1½ oz orange juice
¼ oz triple sec
¾ oz brandy
¾ oz white rum
1 oz dark rum

Shake well over crushed ice in a **shaker**, strain into a large highball glass half-filled with crushed ice, drop the squeezed lime into the glass.

S

SCOTCH SOUR

³/₄–1 oz lemon juice
1 barspoon powdered sugar
¹/₄ oz sugar syrup
2 oz Scotch
stemmed cherry

Shake well over ice cubes in a **shaker**, strain into an old-fashioned glass over ice cubes, garnish with cherry.

SCREWDRIVER

2 oz vodka
3¹/₂ oz orange juice

Stir well over ice cubes in a **collins glass**.

SEPTEMBER MORN

juice of half a lime
1 egg white
2 barspoons powdered sugar
dash grenadine
2 oz white rum

Shake well over ice cubes in a **shaker**, strain into a cock-tail glass.

SHANGHAI

juice of a quarter lime
2 barspoons powdered sugar
dash grenadine
dash anisette
1 1/2 oz dark rum

Shake well over ice cubes in a **shaker**, strain into a cocktail glass.

SHERRY EGGNOG

1 egg yolk
1/4 oz cream
1/4 oz sugar syrup
1 3/4 oz cream sherry
milk
nutmeg

Shake first four ingredients well over ice cubes in a **shaker**, strain into a large highball glass, fill with cold milk, sprinkle with nutmeg.

SHERRY FLIP

1 egg yolk
1/4 oz sugar syrup
3/4 oz cream
1 1/4 oz medium sherry
1/4 oz Cognac
nutmeg

Shake well over ice cubes in a **shaker**, strain into a cocktail glass, sprinkle with nutmeg.

SHIRLEY TEMPLE

4 oz Seven-Up
4 oz ginger ale
dash grenadine

Pour Seven-Up and ginger ale over ice in a **collins glass**, add a dash of grenadine, and stir.

SIDECAR

³/₄ oz lemon juice
¹/₄–³/₄ oz triple sec
1 ¹/₂ oz brandy

Shake well over ice cubes in a **shaker**, strain into a chilled cocktail glass.

SILVER FIZZ

1 oz lemon juice
1 egg white
1 barspoon powdered sugar
¹/₄ oz sugar syrup
2 oz gin
soda

Shake first five ingredients well over ice cubes in a **shaker**, strain into a collins glass over ice, fill with soda.

SILVER JUBILEE

1 1/2 oz cream
1 1/2 oz gin
3/4 oz banana liqueur

Shake well over ice cubes in a **shaker**, strain into a cocktail glass.

SINGAPORE SLING

3/4–1 oz lemon juice
1/4 oz sugar syrup
1 barspoon powdered sugar
1 1/2 oz gin
soda
1/4–3/4 oz cherry
    brandy
stemmed cherry

Shake first four ingredients well over ice cubes in a **shaker**, strain into a collins glass over ice cubes, fill with soda. Carefully pour in cherry brandy, garnish with cherry.

SIR WALTER

3/4 oz lemon juice
1/4 oz triple sec
dash grenadine
3/4 oz white rum
3/4 oz brandy

Shake well over ice cubes in a **shaker**, strain into a chilled cocktail glass.

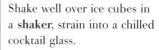

SLOPPY JOE

juice of half a lime
dashes triple sec
dash grenadine
3/4 oz dry vermouth
3/4 oz white rum

Shake well over ice cubes in a **shaker**, strain into a chilled cocktail glass.

SOMBRERO

1 1/2 oz brandy
1/4 oz ruby port
3/4 oz cream

Stir liquors over ice cubes in a **mixing glass**, strain into a sherry glass, carefully top with cream.

SOUTH OF THE BORDER

1/2 lime
1 oz tequila
3/4 oz Tia Maria

Squeeze lime into a **small highball glass**, add ice cubes, pour in liquors, stir well.

SOUTHERN COMFORT SOUR

³/₄ oz lemon juice
¹/₄ oz orange juice
1¹/₂ oz Southern Comfort
stemmed cherry

Shake well over ice cubes in
a **shaker**, strain into an old-
fashioned glass over ice
cubes, garnish with
cherry.

SPRING FEVER (1980)

³/₄ oz lemon juice
³/₄ oz mango syrup
1¹/₂ oz pineapple juice
2 oz blood orange juice

Shake well over ice cubes in
a **shaker**, strain into a collins
glass half-filled with crushed
ice.

SPRITZER

4 oz white wine
soda

Pour wine into a **balloon
wine glass**, add soda.

STINGER

1 1/2 oz brandy
3/4 oz crème de menthe
   (white)

Stir well over crushed ice or ice cubes in a **small highball glass**.

STORMY WEATHER (1980)

3/4 oz Fernet Branca
3/4 oz dry vermouth
1/4 oz crème de menthe
   (white)

Stir over ice cubes in a **small highball glass**.

STRAWBERRY DAIQUIRI

2 large strawberries
juice of a quarter lime
1 barspoon powdered sugar
2 oz white rum
dashes strawberry syrup

Prepare in a **blender** with crushed ice, pour into a cocktail or highball glass.

S

STRAWBERRY MARGARITA

2 large strawberries
juice of a quarter lime
1 barspoon powdered sugar
2 oz tequila
dashes strawberry syrup

Prepare in a **blender** with crushed ice, pour into a cocktail or highball glass.

SUMMER COOLER

1 1/2 oz orange juice
dashes Angostura bitters
Seven-Up

Pour orange juice over ice cubes in a **collins glass**, add dashes Angostura, fill with Seven-Up, stir.

SWEET & HOT (1984)

2 oz milk
3/4 oz cream
3/4 oz Kahlúa
1 1/2 oz dark rum
lemon peel
clove

Heat in a **heat-resistant glass**, add lemon peel and clove.

SWEET SCIENCE (1981)

1½ oz orange juice
¼–¾ oz Drambuie
1½ oz Scotch

Shake well over ice cubes in a **shaker**, strain into a cocktail glass.

SWIMMING POOL (1979)

¾ oz cream
¾ oz coconut cream
2 oz pineapple juice
¾ oz vodka
¾ oz white rum
¼ oz blue curaçao
stemmed cherry
pineapple chunk

Shake first five ingredients well over crushed ice in a **shaker**, strain into a large highball glass over crushed ice, float curaçao on top, garnish with pineapple chunk and cherry.

T

TNT

1 oz Bourbon
1/4–3/4 oz Pernod

Stir over ice cubes in an **old-fashioned glass**. (Add a little water or soda if desired.)

TEQUILA GIMLET

1 oz lemon juice
1/4 oz Rose's lime juice
2 oz white tequila

Shake well over ice cubes in a **shaker**, strain into a chilled cocktail glass. (See also the original Gimlet, made with gin, and the Vodka Gimlet.)

TEQUILA MATADOR

juice of half a lime
1 barspoon powdered sugar
pineapple chunk
1/4 oz triple sec
2 oz tequila

Prepare in a blender with crushed ice, pour into a **small highball glass**.

TEQUILA MOCKINGBIRD

juice of half a lime
1 1/2 oz tequila
1/4 oz crème de menthe
   (green)
soda

Pour first three ingredients
over crushed ice in a **small
highball glass**, drop
squeezed lime into the glass,
add water or soda.

TEQUILA SOUR

3/4 oz lemon juice
1/4–3/4 oz sugar syrup
1 1/2 oz tequila
stemmed cherry

Shake well over ice
cubes in a **shaker**,
strain into a sour
glass, garnish with
cherry.

TEQUILA SUNRISE

lime
dashes grenadine
2 oz tequila
3 1/2 oz orange juice

Squeeze lime wedge into a
large highball glass half-
filled with ice and drop into
the glass, add tequila and
dashes of grenadine, slowly
fill with orange juice.

TEQUINI*

dash Angostura bitters
dashes dry vermouth
2 oz tequila
olive or lemon peel

Stir over ice cubes in a **mixing glass**, strain into a chilled martini glass, add olive or lemon twist.

* Tequila Martini

TIPPERARY

3/4 oz vermouth bianco
1/4 oz green Chartreuse
1 oz Irish whiskey

Stir over ice cubes in a **mixing glass**, strain into a chilled cocktail glass.

TOM & JERRY

1 egg
1–2 barspoons sugar
1 1/2 oz white rum
hot milk
nutmeg

Separate egg yolk from egg white, beat each separately. Add sugar to egg yolk, mix well until sugar dissolves. Place egg white and rum into a **heat-resistant glass**, pour in hot milk, stir well. Sprinkle with nutmeg.

TOM COLLINS*

³/₄–1 oz lemon juice
¹/₄–³/₄ oz sugar syrup
2 oz gin
soda
stemmed cherry
lemon

Stir first three ingredients
well over ice cubes in a
collins glass, fill with soda,
add cherry and lemon slice.

*Tom Collins is the most
famous of collinses.*

COLLINSES MADE WITH OTHER LIQUORS ARE CALLED:

white rum   *Pedro Collins*
dark rum   *Rum Collins*

Canadian whisky   *Captain Collins*
Scotch whisky   *Sandy Collins*
Bourbon whiskey   *Colonel Collins*
Irish whiskey   *Mike Collins*

Cognac   *Pierre Collins*

apple brandy (Calvados)   *Jack Collins*

vodka   *Vodka or Joe Collins*

tequila   *Ruben or Pepito Collins*

Pisco   *Pisco Collins*

TOMATE

1½ oz Ricard
dash grenadine

Stir over ice cubes in an **aperitif glass**, fill with water.

TRICONTINENTAL

¼ oz grenadine
¼ oz crème de cacao
  (brown)
2 oz gold rum

Fill a **Champagne flute** with crushed ice, slowly add ingredients in order listed (so that they float atop each other as in a Pousse Café).

TRINITY

¾ oz vermouth bianco
¾ oz dry vermouth
¾ oz gin
lemon peel

Stir over ice cubes in a **mixing glass**, strain into a chilled martini glass, twist lemon peel over drink.

TROPICAL CHAMPAGNE (1980)

dashes lemon juice
dashes maracuja (passion
    fruit) syrup
3/4 oz orange juice
3/4 oz dark rum
Champagne

Shake first four ingredients
well over ice cubes in a
shaker, strain into a Champagne flute, carefully fill with
Champagne.

V

VELVET HAMMER*

1 oz cream
3/4 oz crème de cacao
    (brown)
3/4 oz vodka

Shake well over ice cubes in a **shaker**, strain into a cocktail glass.

* *Vodka Alexander*

VERMOUTH CASSIS

1/4 oz crème de cassis
1 3/4 oz dry vermouth
soda
lemon peel

Pour crème de cassis and vermouth over ice cubes in an **aperitif glass**, mix, fill with soda, twist lemon peel over drink.

VERMOUTH COCKTAIL*

3/4 oz dry vermouth
3/4 oz vermouth bianco
dash orange bitters

Stir well over ice cubes in a **mixing glass**, strain into a chilled cocktail glass.

* *Half & Half*

VIRGIN MARY

4 oz tomato juice
dashes lemon juice
celery salt
Worcestershire sauce
coarse pepper
Tabasco
celery stalk

Pour tomato juice over ice cubes in a **large highball glass**, season and stir, add celery stalk. (May also be prepared in a **shaker**.)

VODKA GIMLET*

1³/₄ oz Rose's lime juice
1³/₄ oz vodka

Stir well over ice cubes in a **mixing glass**, strain into a chilled cocktail glass.

original version

VODKA GIMLET (SCHUMANN'S)

1 oz lemon juice
1 oz Rose's lime juice
2 oz vodka

Shake well over ice cubes in a **shaker**, strain into a chilled cocktail glass.

VODKA MARTINI*

2 oz vodka
dashes dry vermouth
    (Noilly Prat)
olive or lemon peel

Stir well over ice cubes in a **mixing glass**, strain into a chilled martini glass, add olive or twist lemon peel over drink.

Vodkatini

VODKA SLING

3/4–1 oz lemon juice
1 barspoon powdered sugar
2 oz vodka
soda
1/4 oz cherry brandy
stemmed cherry
lemon

Shake first three ingredients well over ice cubes in a **shaker**, strain into a collins glass over ice cubes, fill with soda, slowly top with cherry brandy, stir, garnish with cherry and lemon wedge.

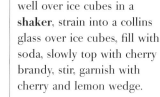

VODKA SOUR

3/4 oz lemon juice
1/4–3/4 oz sugar syrup
1 1/2 oz vodka
stemmed cherry

Shake well over ice cubes in a **shaker**, strain into a sour glass, garnish with cherry.

VODKA STINGER

1¼ oz vodka
¼ oz crème de menthe
   (white)

Stir well over ice cubes or
crushed ice in a **small highball glass**

VOLCANO

¾ oz raspberry liqueur
¾ oz blue curaçao
Champagne
orange peel

Pour liqueurs into a **Champagne flute**, fill with ice-cold
Champagne, twist orange
peel over drink. (Raspberry
liqueur and curaçao may
be heated, lit to flame, and
extinguished with
Champagne.)

VOLGA VOLGA (1979)

2 oz vodka
¼ oz crème de menthe
(green)
tonic water

Stir liquors over crushed ice in a **small highball glass**, fill with tonic water.

W

WALDORF-ASTORIA EGGNOG

2 egg yolks
$^1/_4$ oz sugar syrup
$^3/_4$ oz tawny port
$1^1/_2$ oz Bourbon
$3^1/_2$ oz milk
$^1/_4$ oz cream
nutmeg

Shake well over ice cubes in a **shaker**, strain into a large highball glass over ice cubes, sprinkle with nutmeg.

WARD EIGHT

$^3/_4$ oz lemon juice
1 barspoon powdered sugar
dash grenadine
$1^3/_4$ oz Bourbon
stemmed cherry

Shake over ice cubes in a **shaker**, strain into a sour glass, garnish with cherry.

WEDDING BELLS COCKTAIL

$^3/_4$ oz orange juice
$^3/_4$ oz gin
$^3/_4$ oz Dubonnet
$^1/_4$ oz cherry brandy

Shake well over ice cubes in a **shaker**, strain into a chilled cocktail glass.

W

WEST INDIAN PUNCH

juice of half a lime
1 oz pineapple juice
1 oz orange juice
3/4 oz banana liqueur
2 oz dark rum
nutmeg

Shake over crushed ice in a **shaker**, strain into a collins glass, fill with crushed ice, sprinkle with nutmeg.

WHISKEY HOT TODDY

3/4 oz lemon juice
1/4 oz sugar syrup
1 1/2 oz Bourbon
lemon
clove

Heat in a **heat-resistant glass**, fill with hot water, add lemon slice spiked with clove.

WHISKEY SOUR*

3/4 oz lemon juice
1 barspoon powdered sugar
1/4 oz sugar syrup
1 1/2 oz Bourbon
stemmed cherry

Shake well over ice cubes in a **shaker**, strain into a sour glass, add cherry.

Whiskey Sour variations: Scotch Sour, Jack Sour, Wild Turkey Sour

WHITE CLOUD

³/₄ oz cream
2 oz pineapple juice
³/₄ oz crème de cacao
    (white)
1 ¹/₂ oz vodka

Shake well over ice cubes in a **shaker**, strain into a large highball glass over crushed ice.

WHITE LADY

³/₄ oz lemon juice
1 egg white
1 barspoon powdered sugar
¹/₄–³/₄ oz triple sec
1 ¹/₂ oz gin

Shake well over ice cubes in a **shaker**, strain into a chilled cocktail glass.

WHITE RUSSIAN

1 oz vodka
³/₄ oz Kahlúa
cream

Stir liquors over ice cubes in a **mixing glass**, strain into a sherry glass, top with lightly whipped cream.

YELLOW BIRD NO. 1

juice of half a lime
1 ¼ oz orange juice
¼ oz Tia Maria
1 oz white rum
1 oz dark rum
mint sprig
stemmed cherry

Shake over crushed ice in a shaker, strain into a **large highball glass** half-filled with crushed ice, garnish with mint sprig and cherry.

YELLOW BIRD NO. 2

juice of half a lime
1 ¼ oz orange juice
¼ oz Galliano
1 oz white rum
1 oz dark rum
mint sprig
stemmed cherry

Shake over crushed ice in a **shaker**, strain into a collins glass half-filled with crushed ice, garnish with mint sprig and cherry.

YELLOW BOXER (1981)

¾ oz lemon juice
¾ oz Rose's lime juice
¾ oz orange juice
¼ oz Galliano
1 ¾ oz tequila

Shake well over ice cubes in a **shaker**, strain into a chilled cocktail glass.

Y

YELLOW FEVER (1982)

2 oz pineapple juice
¹/₄ oz lemon juice
¹/₄ oz Galliano
1 ¹/₂ oz vodka

Shake well over ice cubes in a **shaker**, strain into a large highball glass over crushed ice.

YELLOW PARROT

³/₄ oz yellow Chartreuse
³/₄ oz apricot brandy
¹/₄ oz anisette

Stir over ice cubes in a **mixing glass**, strain into a chilled cocktail glass.

ZICO (1986)

juice of a quarter lime
3/4 oz coconut cream
2 oz papaya juice
1 oz white rum
1 oz cachaça

Shake well over crushed ice in a **shaker**, strain into a large highball glass over crushed ice.

ZOMBIE

1 1/4 oz lemon juice
dashes grenadine
3/4 oz blood orange juice
3/4 oz Cherry Heering
3/4 oz white rum
2 oz dark rum
3/4 oz high-proof
    dark rum

Shake over ice cubes in a shaker, strain into a **large highball glass** over crushed ice.

Main Cocktail and Drink Categories

Cocktails are commonly divided into two categories according to volume: **short drinks** (up to 3½ oz) and **tall drinks** (up to 8½ oz or even more).

But a multitude of categories are defined by cocktail ingredients. Many bartending books from the 1930s list more than thirty categories! Many of them, of course, are no longer familiar or commonly served in bars. **I consider the ones in the following list the most important and up-to-date.**

Note that I place aperitifs and digestifs at the top. The bartender can and should make **recommendations** to his guests—making recommendations is critical to the reputation of a bar—and to me these cocktails, served before and after mealtime, are the **true stars of bar cocktails.**

1. **Aperitifs** / Before-Dinner Cocktails
   a) All-American Favorites
   b) Aperitifs of Southern Europe

2. **Digestifs** / After-Dinner Cocktails

3. **Restorative Drinks**
   Corpse Revivers, Pick-Me-Up Cocktails, & Hangover Drinks

4. **Champagne Cocktails**

5. **Sours, Fizzes, Collinses**

6. **Eggnogs & Flips**

7. **Highballs**

8. **Juleps**

9. **Hot Drinks & Coffee Drinks**

10. **Bowls**

11. **Punches**

12. **Coladas**

13. **Nonalcoholic Cocktails & Drinks**

1. APERITIFS

Aperitifs—also known as **before-dinner drinks** or **starters**—should whet the appetite and make the time before dinner pass pleasantly, but they should never suppress hunger or numb the taste buds.

I divide them into two categories:

A) ALL-AMERICAN FAVORITES: These are the historically classic cocktails of the American bar and should be available in any bar whether they are listed on the drink menu or not.

A few examples: The number-one aperitif—the king of cocktails—is the cocktail of the blue hour: the dry **Martini** and all its variations. Next is the **Manhattan**, the **Old-Fashioned**, **Bronx**, **Sidecar**, and **White Lady** (favorites among women but by no means limited to the early evening hours).

B) APERITIFS OF SOUTHERN EUROPE: Wine-based spirits and bitters from the southern part of Europe are particularly suitable as aperitifs. Classic aperitifs are: sherry (dry, medium, or sweet), vermouth (dry, bianco, or rosso), Campari, Cynar, and Dubonnet.

Many of these aperitif spirits can also be enjoyed unmixed, but Campari and vermouth are particularly good as mixers. They form the basis of many cocktails and are the harmonizing element in many others (for example, **Campari Cocktail**, **Cynar Cocktail**, **Americano**, **Negroni**).

In the southern parts of Europe aperitif spirits with a bitter taste or flavored with anise are especially popular (for example, **Pernod**, **Pastis**, **Cynar**, **Campari**, and **Ouzo**). They are often served mixed with soda or water. And of course most Champagne cocktails may also be served as an aperitif.

Because there are fewer and fewer drinkers of hard liquor and because drinking customs have changed, the **Spritzer** (white wine with soda) follows close on the heels of the dry Martini in popularity, as does the **small (short) beer**, which is enjoyed in Germany and elsewhere as an **aperitif**

Every bartender in the world—as good ones already know—should see to it that prior to a meal no guests overburden their stomach and tax their taste buds to the point that they would have to wait hours before they could truly enjoy their meal.

Serving an aperitif means preparing a guest's palate for a meal by serving a beverage that will allow him or her to sit down to eat feeling refreshed and hungry.

2. DIGESTIFS

Digestifs, or **after-dinner-drinks**, bring closure to a meal and often are also enjoyed as a nightcap.

There are two possibilities in serving digestifs (besides having them neat):

1. Mixed spirits:
   B & P (brandy and port)
   B & B (brandy and Bénédictine)
   Black Russian (vodka and Kahlúa)

2. Other combinations using liquors, juices, and so forth in dessert cocktails.
   Many such cocktails are world-famous:
   Brandy Alexander
   Grasshopper
   Golden Cadillac
   Golden Dream
   White Russian

3. RESTORATIVE DRINKS

The distinction between **pick-me-ups**, **hangover drinks**, and **corpse revivers** is rather fluid. These are all drinks and cocktails that are intended to have a restorative effect. A simple cup of tea or coffee or a glass of cola or mineral water is helpful for many guests. Often an aspirin or two can make the best medicine.

These cocktails are not classified by their ingredients. Classics among them are the **Virgin Mary**, **Bloody Mary**, **Bullshot**, **Pink Gin**, and the **Corpse Revivers** concocted by Frank Meier of the Ritz Bar in Paris.

Every bartender should have his own prescription for his "patients."

But sometimes it's better simply to limit the amount of alcohol consumed before it's too late.

4. CHAMPAGNE COCKTAILS

In bar terminology the sparkling wine used in cocktails is called "mixing Champagne." But just because it's used for mixing doesn't mean it should be of poor quality—and it should always be brut! Some bars have become very famous because of their Champagne cocktails, such as the concoction known as the Bellini served at Harry's Bar in Venice. I separate Champagne cocktails into several groups:

1. Neat spirits into which sparkling wine is added. Most suitable for this are fruit brandies (such as poire Williams).

2. Liquors (such as gin, vodka, brandy) mixed with liqueurs and dashes of juice and syrups, with sparkling wine added in. Careful with syrups and liqueurs—just one more dash can often be too much!

3. Liquors mixed with fresh-squeezed juices and topped off with sparkling wine.

4. Juices and pureed fruits mixed with sparkling wine. A bit of lemon juice must be sprinkled on top of pureed fruits to prevent them from taking on any unappetizing dark color.

5. SOURS, FIZZES, COLLINSES

SOURS: My favorite drinks are sours made from the original cocktail ingredients:

lemon juice

sugar

liquors

Sometimes **a little orange juice** is added to sours, but I find this unnecessary. Sours can be mixed from almost any spirits (only in a shaker). The best known are: **Whiskey Sour**, **Gin Sour**, **Rum Sour**, and **Pisco Sour**. As a rule, sours are served in a sour glass garnished with a stemmed maraschino cherry, but they may also be served on the rocks in a tumbler or an old-fashioned glass.

FIZZES

Main ingredients:

lemon juice

sugar

liquors

soda

Fizzes are sours that are shaken and then filled with soda. Instead of sugar other sweeteners, such as syrup or honey, may be used.

In contrast to collinses, fizzes are primarily gin drinks with variations: **Gin Fizz**, **Silver Fizz**, **Golden Fizz**, **Royal Fizz**, **Orange Fizz**, **Morning Glory Fizz**, and **New Orleans Fizz** (**Ramos Fizz**). Also well known are the **Vodka Fizz**, **Brandy Fizz**, **Rum Fizz**, and **Whisk(e)y Fizz**.

COLLINSES

Main ingredients:

> **lemon juice**
> **sugar**
> **liquors**
> **soda**

Collinses are tall sours and are related to fizzes. In contrast, however, they are stirred in a drinking glass and garnished with a lemon wedge and a cherry. Like sours and fizzes, collinses are excellent refreshment on hot summer nights. The best-known collins is the **Tom Collins** (lemon juices, sugar syrup, and gin).

Personally, I prefer fizzes over collinses. Shaking the ingredients to prepare a fizz (as opposed to stirring them in preparing a collins) is the better method for making a perfectly blended drink.

Nearly every liquor has its collins. (See page 187.)

6. EGGNOGS & FLIPS

EGGNOGS: This is a cocktail group that is truly historic (although it is not terribly popular at present).

Main ingredients:

    egg yolk

    sugar (or other sweetener)

    spirits (liqueurs, brandies)

    cream (or milk)

Eggnogs are well shaken over ice cubes in a shaker and served in a cocktail glass with nutmeg sprinkled on top. The primary liquors for eggnogs, after which the various recipes are also named, are **sherry**, **Madeira**, **ruby port**, **brandy**, **rum**, and **whisk(e)y**. Liqueurs may also be used either alone or in combination with a liquor.

FLIPS

Main ingredients:

egg yolk

sugar

spirits (liqueurs, brandies)

Flips and eggnogs are similar. Flips are usually made without milk or cream. (I add a **small amount of cream** into flips. A combination of egg, sugar, and spirits is, in my view, not harmonious enough.)

Mostly wine-based liquors are suitable for flips (brandy, sherry, Madeira, and port), but rum and whisk(e)y may be used as well.

The best liqueurs are apricot brandy, cherry brandy, and triple sec.

Famous flips are: the **New York Flip**, **Brandy Flip**, **Sherry Flip**, **Porto Flip**, and **Champagne Flip**.

7. HIGHBALLS

Main ingredients:

liquor

water

sodas (ginger ale, tonic water, bitter lemon, or flavored sodas may be used.)

Highballs are drinks made of liquor (such as gin, vodka, whisk(e)y, cognac, etc.) to which soda or water is added. They are prepared in a drinking glass over ice.

Highballs are served in a collins glass (or in a large highball glass) over ice, often with a lemon or orange twist. A splash of bitters nicely rounds off the highball. The **Bourbon Highball** (Bourbon and ginger ale) is a well-known drink.

8. JULEPS

Main ingredients:

mint

liquor

Juleps are among the oldest mixed drinks in the world. They are said to have originated in the South.

The most important requirement for making a good julep is aromatic mint. Mint that grows in sunny climates naturally has a much more pungent aroma.

Juleps are prepared in a drinking glass. Per drink approximately 10 mint leaves are placed into a collins glass, 1–2 sugar cubes are added, and with an iced-tea spoon or a barspoon the mint leaves are pressed so that the moisture and aroma from the leaves combines with the sugar. Some prefer to remove the pressed leaves from the glass, but I like to leave them in. The glass is then filled halfway with crushed ice, the liquor is poured in and stirred well, and the glass is filled to the rim with ice. To finish I add a sprig of mint sprinkled with powdered sugar.

The best-known juleps are:

Mint Julep "Southern Style" (Bourbon Julep) and **Champagne Julep.**

The world-famous **Mojito** is a rum Julep.

Fruits do not belong in a julep!

9. HOT DRINKS & COFFEE DRINKS

Hot bar drinks are **not only for wintertime**, although of course they are more frequently ordered during the colder months of the year. Hot alcoholic drinks are prepared in heat-resistant glasses, and the **alcohol must only be heated**—it should never be allowed to boil.

Alcohol can be combined with

hot coffee

hot tea (Grog)

hot water (Grog, Toddy)

hot wine

hot milk

and with **hot cream** too!

HOT COFFEE DRINKS

Hot drinks with coffee are the most common and well known of all hot bar drinks.

In these the liquor is usually heated with sugar (often brown sugar) and then the glass is filled with hot coffee, stirred well, and often topped with whipped cream. **Without the sugar the whipped cream will disperse and sink!**

The best-known hot coffee drink is **Irish Coffee**.

GROG

Ingredients:

lemon juice

sugar

liquor (heated!)

hot water or hot tea

aromatic fruit and spice (lemon peel, orange peel, cloves for flavor)

Suitable liquors for grog are arak and/or rum, but gin, brandy, and whisk(e)y (**Hot Toddy**) are also excellent.

Heat the liquor in a heat-resistant glass, fill with hot tea or water, add fruit and spice.

HOT PUNCH

Ingredients:

liquor

juice

sugar

water or juice

aromatic spices

Heat the ingredients in a heat-resistant glass, add spices. Juice can be used instead of water. Punches are **tall drinks** and **may also be served cold**.

MULLED WINE

Usually made with red wine, mulled wine can also be made with white wine. Aromatic spices for mulled wine are cinnamon, clove, lemon peel, and orange peel. Heat the wine in a heat-resistant glass (do not boil), and add the aromatic ingredients.

TODDY

Ingredients:

liquor

sugar or honey

water or juice

The toddy is similar to punch, but it is a **short drink**. A hot toddy is prepared in a heat-resistant glass. It **may also be served cold**. The best-known toddy is the **Whisk(e)y Hot Toddy**.

COLD COFFEE DRINKS

Cold coffee is not just cold coffee. Cold coffee over ice, with ice cream, and cold coffee with alcohol—but not too much—are truly invigorating stimulants.

Try a **Black Rose**—cold coffee with white rum and sugar sprinkled with ground cloves and cinnamon.

Cold coffee must have sugar to reveal its mysterious powers, and only with sugar is it palatable. More than once have I declared my fondness for espresso, especially down to the very last sugary drop with a little Spanish brandy added to it.

A bar should offer coffee and, better yet, espresso—even outside of Italy!

10. BOWLS

Ingredients:
liquor
wine, sparkling wine
fruits
herbs
water

Even though a bowl is not exactly a bar drink, it is still wise to know how to prepare one. **There are two kinds of preparation:**

a) Bowls that are prepared and served immediately.

b) Bowls that are covered and set aside for a few hours or days to chill. In this case the liquors, wines, fruits, and herbs are combined in the bowl. Then just before serving, the bowl containing this fruit, herb, and alcohol mixture is filled with wine or sparkling wine.

Soda (water, mineral water, ginger ale, etc.) can be added instead to the base of alcohol, herbs, and fruits.

The bowl is often there to greet us in Italian aperitif bars, where it is known as **"aperitivo de la casa."**

11. PUNCHES

The most famous fruit punch of all originated in the 1700s: **Planter's Punch**. There is an enormous variety of Planter's Punches, but each one is basically a mixed drink containing **several fruit juices and rum**.

In most areas of the Caribbean, Planter's Punch is mixed with dark rum; only in the French Antilles is white rum used for a punch known as Planteur, usually mixed with lime juice, orange juice, maracuja (passion fruit) juice, or grapefruit juice.

A specialty of the French Antilles is the Petite Punch or Ponche Blanche—one part white rum, one part cane sugar syrup, lime, and ice.

In the fishing ports along the coast of Martinique, Ponche Blanche is consumed in a simpler but more potent formula: a water glass filled with white rum, two spoonfuls of brown sugar, and a quarter of a lime. A time-honored aid against a hangover the next morning: salted dry fish.

Fruit punches can be prepared with a wide variety of seasonable tropical fruit juices.

12. COLADAS

Ingredients:

coconut cream

cream

juice

liquor

In the last few years coladas have become one of the most popular mixed drinks, and the most popular colada of all is the **Piña Colada**.

The basic ingredients in the Piña Colada are:

rum

pineapple juice

coconut cream

Interesting coladas that are completely different can be created by using other kinds of juice combined with various syrups or liqueurs. Variations on the recipe using Galliano (vanilla liqueur) or Tia Maria, Cognac, cachaça, or Kahlúa can make for some tasty new drinks.

Real coconut cream is made from the first pressing of a coconut and has a fat content of about 35 percent. Coconut milk is a mixture of this cream with the liquid from the second pressing of a coconut and warm water. Coconut milk has a fat content of 10 to 20 percent. (The product sold in markets called "coconut cream" is often actually coconut milk.)

13. NONALCOHOLIC COCKTAILS & DRINKS

Ingredients:
   juices
   fruits
   syrups
   milk
   water & sodas

No bar can do without offering a wide selection of non-alcoholic drinks (almost exclusively tall drinks). The creativity of the bartender may be boundless in making these drinks. It is of course best to use fresh-squeezed juices and fresh fruits in preparing them whenever possible.

The classic bar, however, is certainly not a fruit and vegetable stand.

Along with juices and fruits, nonalcoholic drink recipes require various syrups, sodas (tonic, bitter lemon, ginger ale), and lemonade.

Until recently the selection of nonalcoholic drinks in classic bars was rather limited—just one or two mineral waters (still and sparkling) and fresh juices—usually orange, grapefruit, and lemon juice. Equally paltry was the selection of mixed drinks, which were limited to tomato juice preparations (**Virgin Mary**) and the **Sportsman**. Now, however, almost all tropical fruits have become available in the form of juices, nectars, and syrups, and nonalcoholic mixed drinks made from them have become a big hit. With a little imagination some delicious drinks can be made with these.

It is important to keep in mind that ingredients such as syrup and cream must be handled especially carefully. Fresh juices and pureed fruits should of course be **used immediately**, because when absolutely fresh they are much more than a mere thirst quencher—they are a **stimulating refreshment that is also healthy**.

COCKTAIL COMPONENTS

DISTILLATES FROM WINE

The best-known distillations of wine are the famous brandies of France, **Cognac** and **Armagnac**, but Spain, Italy, Portugal, Greece, Germany, the United States, and South America also produce excellent brandies. As a rule, the different types of brandy made in individual countries are 80° proof; the details are controlled by national regulations.

Marc and **grappa**, unlike other brandies, are distilled not from wine but from the skins and husks of pressed grapes.

COGNAC

Cognac is the best known and most famous of the world's brandies.

The Charente and Charente Maritime departments, north of Bordeaux, are the source of Cognac. Only brandy from this legally delimited district in France may be labeled Cognac. The chalky soil, the climate, and the proximity to the ocean present a unique advantage for the vineyards, which produce a thin acidic white wine, unattractive on its own, but ideal for distillation into brandy. The Cognac region, known simply as Charente, after the river, is the largest area of vineyards, which are planted with three grape varieties: Ugni Blanc, Colombard, and Folle Blanche.

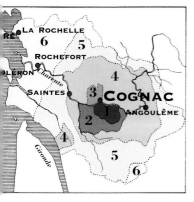

1. *Grande Champagne*
2. *Petite Champagne*
3. *Les Borderies*
4. *Fins Bois*
5. *Bons Bois*
6. *Bois Ordinaires*

Charente is subdivided into different districts with different geological and physical characteristics: **"bois"** (forest areas), **"champs"** (fields), and **"champagne"** (open fields).

(Note: *Champagne* on a Cognac label has nothing to do with sparkling wine.)

THE SIX DIVISIONS OF CHARENTE

1. **Grande Champagne** is the area of premium quality. From the grapes grown in this district the finest, most aromatic Cognacs are distilled, which, because they develop slowly, are used primarily in blends given lengthy aging. Cognacs exclusively from this area can be labeled "Grande Fine Champagne." Fifteen percent of the wines that are used in Cognac production come from this area.

2. **Petite Champagne**: Twenty percent of the wines that go into Cognac come from this second-best area. A blend of Cognacs from Petite Champagne and Grande Champagne—if it contains a minimum of 50 percent of the latter—can be labeled "Fine Champagne."

3. **Les Borderies**: The wines of this region make a mild Cognac with a rich bouquet. They make up only 5 percent of Cognac production all together.

4. **Fins Bois**: The greatest percentage of Cognac is distilled from the wines grown in this area—approximately 40 percent. These are strong, quickly aging Cognacs, and the chief component of Cognacs not given lengthy aging.

5. **Bons Bois**: Approximately 15 percent of the wines used in Cognac production are from this area; strong brandies, most not of terribly high quality.

6. **Bois Ordinaires**: This area accounts for about 3 percent of all Cognac production.

DISTILLING COGNAC A tradition dating from the seventeenth century forms the foundation of all Cognac production. The wine is double-distilled in traditional pot stills (*alambic charentais*) that may be filled with up to 660 gallons.

The first distillation produces a liquid called *brouillis*, which has an alcoholic content of about 60° proof (or 30% by volume). This is distilled again to produce a clear, raw young spirit, known as *bonne chauffe*. In the second distillation, the beginning and the end of the process—the "heads and tails"—are kept separate; both may be distilled again into unrefined brandy. The middle runnings (*coeur*), at about 140° proof, yield the best and purest quality.

AGING All Cognac is aged for several years (at least two for sale in the United States, but often twenty or more) in oak casks (*barriques*). These wood containers are porous, which exposes the Cognac to slow, continued oxidation, and the brandy also picks up color, tannin, and taste from the oak. This process transforms a harsh distillate into a smooth, harmonious spirit—undesirable flavors vanish while desirable flavors concentrate. Old Cognacs are not necessarily dark in color; in fact, it is common practice to adjust the color of Cognacs with a small

amount of caramel to maintain consistency of appearance in the bottle.

STRENGTH The alcohol content of raw Cognac is 140° proof, but it diminishes slowly in the cask. Before bottling, it is normally diluted with distilled water and "faible" (low-proof Cognac) to lower it to a minimum 80° proof.

Aside from a very few exceptions, Cognac is always a blend of single Cognacs of various maturities, sources, and vintages. The blending is done so that the character and quality that distinguishes each brand is assured over a long period of time.

COGNAC LABELS carry various markings—initials, stars, phrases—from which the minimum age of the Cognac can be inferred. It would be impossible to list here the entire multitude of descriptions allowed, but the following are the most common. The date specified always refers to the number of years the youngest of the ingredients has been in the cask.

Cognacs that have been aged for a minimum of **two years** counting from 1 April following the distillation can be labeled ★★★ (three—or more—stars); V.S.; V.S.P.

a minimum of **four years** can be labeled V.S.O.P.; V.O.

a minimum of **six years** can be labeled Extra; Napoléon; X.O.

There is no official designation for Cognacs aged over six years, and proprietary names—Triomphe, Très Vénérable, Paradis, etc.—are often used.

Some famous brands of Cognac are:

Bisquit—80° proof; available as:
★★★; V.S.O.P.; Napoléon; Extra Vieille

Camus—80° proof, large agricultural firm; available as:
Grand V.S.O.P.; Napoléon; X.O.; Extra

Courvoisier—80° proof; available as:
V.S.; V.S.O.P.; Napoléon; X.O.

Delamain—80° proof; Delamain Cognacs are among the best although Delamain possesses no vineyards of its own. The wines for the Cognacs are always purchased. Available as: Pale & Dry; Vesper; Très Vénérable; Réserve de la Famille

A. Hardy—80° proof, family enterprise; Cognacs include:
"Red Corner" Fine Cognac V.S.; V.S.O.P. Fine Champagne; "Les Noces d'Or" Grande Champagne Cognac

Hennessy—80° proof, a major producer; available as:
V.S.; V.S.O.P. Privilège; X.O.; Paradis

Hine S. A.—80° proof; available as:
V.S.O.P.; Antique; Triomphe; Family Reserve

Martell—80° proof, one of the largest Cognac manufacturers; available as:
V.S. Grande Fine; Médaillon V.S.O.P.; Cordon Bleu; X.O. Cordon Suprême

Otard—80° proof; available as:
V.S.O.P.; Napoléon; S.O.; Extra

Rémy Martin—80° proof; among others, their Cognacs include:
V.S.; Fine Petite Champagne (★★★); V.S.O.P.; Extra
Perfection; Louis XIII Grande Champagne

ARMAGNAC

A worthy but less famous brother of Cognac, Armagnac is actually much older than Cognac. The first document mentioning it dates from the fifteenth century (1461). Outside France, Armagnac is not as well known as it should be—only a few kinds are available, and so its audience is small. And Armagnac connoisseurs are very few.

It is produced in the region of Gascony in certain areas within the Gers, Landes, and Lot-et-Garonne departments. Traditionally Armagnac has been continually distilled in the small, inefficient *alambic armagnaçaise* from the thin white wines of **three grape varieties**—Ugni Blanc, Colombard, and Folle Blanche—although for the last several years the pot still used in Cognac method has also been permitted. Armagnac is typically richer than Cognac but has less finesse.

THE THREE CULTIVATION AREAS OF ARMAGNAC

1. **Bas Armagnac** (sandy soil): the best and the largest portion of production (approximately 50 percent)
2. **Ténarèze** (clay soil): 40 percent of production
3. **Haut Armagnac** (chalky soil): 5 percent of production

Any one of these apellations may appear on the label of a bottle of Armagnac, but printed on most labels is either "Appellation Armagnac" or "Appellation Bas Armagnac." The latter indicates premium-quality product comparable to a Grande Champagne Cognac.

As a rule, the distillates from the three regions (but sometimes from only two) and of various vintages are blended together to maintain consistency. Unlike Cognac, Armagnac bottlings may carry vintage dates.

Following are the most important of the indications of age:

a minimum of **three years**:
V.S.; ★★★

a minimum of **four years**:
V.O.; V.S.O.P.; Réserve

a minimum of **five years**:
Extra; Napoléon; X.O.; Vieille Réserve;

a minimum of **ten years**: Hors d'age

Famous brands of Armagnac:

Clés des Ducs—80° proof, among others; available as: Extra Grande Réserve; Grande Réserve; V.S.O.P.

Janneau—80° proof, among others; available as: Tradition; Très Vieille Réserve

Marquis de Montesquiou—82° proof, among others; available as: Grande Réserve; X.O.

Samalens—80° proof, among others; available as: V.S.O.P.; Vieille Relique; Cuvée Ami Réserve (Bas Armagnac)

BRANDY

SPANISH BRANDY For over a hundred years brandy has been produced in Spain. Although brandy was once merely a by-product of sherry production, the Spanish are now the largest consumers of brandy in the world. Spanish brandies are comparatively full in flavor, slightly sweet, and can be of exceptional quality. The majority of them are produced by the large sherry houses in Jerez de la Frontera; the grapes, however, come from the region known as La Mancha, south of Madrid—so it is no wonder that they frequently are made by the elaborate "solera method" (see Sherry).

Aging data: The designations for the aging period in the cask, from youngest to oldest, are as follows:

Brandy de Jerez Solera (the youngest salable brandies), Solera Reserva, Solera Gran Reserva.

Some brands are:

Bobadilla—103; Extra Etiqueta Negra; Reserva Gran Capitan

Cardenal Mendoza—Solera Gran Reserva, 90° proof

Pedro Domecq—Carlos I, Gran Reserva, 80° proof; Carlos III, Solera Reservada, 80° proof; Fundador, 76° proof; Marques de Domecq

Gran Duque d'Alba–Solera Gran Reserva, 80° proof

Osborne–Veterano, 73° proof; Conde de Osborne

Lepanto–80° proof

ITALIAN BRANDY
Generally 80° proof.

Buton in Bologna makes, among other products, exceptional brandies: Buton Vecchia Romagna; Etichetta Nera; Etichetta Oro.

From the firm Stock of Turin: Stock Ardente (strong brandy); Riserva Speciale (aged brandy); "84" Dieci Anni

PORTUGUESE BRANDY
The Portuguese term for brandy is aguardente. This brandy is aged in old port wine casks, because the main product of most Portuguese brandy manufacturers is port wine. Ribero & Ferreira, for example, produces Aguardente 1920, 80° proof.

GREEK BRANDY
Metaxa is the most famous Greek brandy. It is distilled from red grapes, sweetened, and flavored with natural aromatic substances. It is 80° proof and is available in various grades of quality, most of which are not only clearly distinguished by their age but also by their taste and character:

Metaxa ★★★★★ (five stars);
Golden Amphora (seven stars);
Grand Olympian Reserve;
Centenary

GERMAN BRANDY

The Versailles Treaty forbade the use of the term *Cognac* for German brandies. So they had to make do with the earlier term *Weinbrand,* coined by Hugo Asbach, which has since been taken up by European Community regulations and defined.

German brandies may use wines from all countries within the European Community; quality-conscious producers purchase base wines for distillation or unaged brandies from famous brandy-producing areas such as Charente or Gascogne.

Regardless of whether a firm produces its own brandy or purchases it, it must be distilled into refined brandy. A brandy labeled "Deutscher Weinbrand" (no German base wines are required) must carry an official inspection number and be at least 76° proof.

The brandy must be aged in wooden casks for a minimum of six months; brandies that have been aged for more than twelve months may carry the description "Old Brandy Wine" *Alter Weinbrand* or the initials V.S.O.P.

Famous brands:
Asbach Uralt
Jacobi
Dujardin
Schlarachberg
Bols
Mariacron (the market leader)
Chantré

U.S. BRANDY

Two-thirds of the brandy consumed in the United States is produced in that country, and virtually all of it comes from California. Brandy from that state is mostly distilled from wines made from table or raisin grapes and is clean, light, and somewhat fruity. In recent years small artisan producers have succeeded in using Cognac-style pot stills to produce tiny amounts of very high quality, notably aromatic brandy.

Principal California brandy producers:

E & J: This Gallo label accounts for almost half of all California brandy produced.

Christian Brothers
Korbel
Paul Masson

Germain-Robin: a tiny but top-quality California producer

SOUTH AMERICAN BRANDIES

Pisco, the national drink of Chile, is rich in tradition.

The base wine, made primarily from Muscat grapes, grows north of Santiago de Chile in precisely demarcated official regions. A period of aging in oak or clay jars follows the distillation process.

The most popular in Chile—with annual sales of 23 million bottles—is Pisco Control in La Serena.

Other South American countries that manufacture brandy include Argentina, Bolivia, and Peru.

Pisco Sour is the best-known Pisco bar drink.

Well-known brands:

Control Gran Pisco—Gran Pisco, Chile, 86° proof
Pisco Capel—Chile, 86° proof

MARC AND GRAPPA

Brandy does not have to be distilled from wine; it can also be distilled from the remaining skins, husks, and stems of grapes that have been pressed to make wine.

Marc from France and grappa from Italy are well known. These "vintners' brandies," formerly known as "poor man's brandy," have become increasingly popular as digestifs.

MARC Light in color, bright, also yellowish, 80° to 90° proof. Famous types are:

Marc de Bourgogne–strong and aromatic

Marc de Champagne–light, delicate, and often mild

GRAPPA Italy has long had a tradition of grappa production. This clear, fiery, pungent spirit used to be regarded as little more than a raw, rustic liquor. But in recent years many wine producers have begun to bottle grappas made from various regions, individual vineyards, and even specific grape varieties. Some of these fashionable grappas are flavored, and many come in specially designed bottles. Most grappa is not aged, but a few are matured for two to four years in wooden casks. **The type of wood influences the bouquet and color**–cherry wood adds a sweet nuance, oak gives dryness, etc. The best grappas come from Venice and Friuli (regions backed by a long tradition). **Nardini** is a well-known brand.

DISTILLATES FROM GRAIN

The following lists spirits that are made from grain. This categorization is not precise in every instance. Differing national regulations and the guidelines of the European Community permit all the spirits listed here to be described as grain distillates (except whisk(e)y and rye) as well as the so-called agricultural alcohols, made, for example, from molasses, potatoes, and so forth. A number of superior products within these individual types are nevertheless based on grain alcohol.

Generally the grains used for distillations are barley, wheat, rye, and corn, and less frequently oat and rice.

Gin
Aquavit
Whisk(e)y
Vodka

GIN

Gin is a highly distilled spirit that is based on **grain**. Its bouquet comes from **junipers**, **coriander**, **herbs**, and **spices**.

As is true of all great spirits, gin, the most popular bar liquor, requires first-class ingredients: a very pure spirit base and a blend of select herbs and spices from all over the world. These include, for example, coriander from Mexico, lemon and orange (rinds) from southern Europe, licorice from England, angelica and juniper from Germany, orrisroot from Italy, almonds, cardamom, and cassia bark from Southeast Asia, and anise from France. **Especially important is pure, soft water**, and of course exceptionally talented specialists who know how to produce a quality gin. There are two methods of distillation: either the rising alcohol fumes are conducted directly over fresh juniper berries and other herbs to absorb their aroma and flavor, or juniper berries and other herbs are mixed with a grain mash and they are distilled together. Gin is stored in glass, earthenware, or stainless steel, but does not mature in these containers. The storage time serves only to harmonize the product. European Community regulations stipulate that gin must be a minimum of 75° proof, and dry gin must be at least 80° proof.

The history of gin is adventuresome. It has seen its highs and lows, and the bad reputation it has suffered has continued in some places to this very day. Gin was once considered the "bad boy" of liquors: cheaply made alcohol that could be gotten anywhere.

It all started with a Dutch professor of medicine. Franciscus de la Boe is generally considered to be the inventor of the

When my patients require spirits—

I prescribe

de KuYPER'S

Heart Label

HOLLANDS

botanically aromatic alcohol known today as gin. He named the drink "Essence de Genièvre," mainly because of its strong juniper bouquet; later it was called "Geneva," and after that "Genever."

Originally intended for medicinal purposes—mainly for Dutch travelers to the West Indies—Genever became familiar in England at the time that William III of Orange assumed the British throne (1689). He wanted to curb imports, especially from France, so he imposed extremely high duties and taxes on imports. As a countermeasure he permitted his subjects to distill Genever, which he had "brought from home." Over time, Genever, a difficult word for the British, became known in England as gin.

British distillers soon were producing gin in their own stills. At the beginning of the eighteenth century drinks similar to gin frequently caused infirmity or even death. Gin was said to pave the way to unemployment, poverty, and despair.

More than a hundred million liters of the cheapest alcohol were manufactured then in Great Britain and even given to children. Cheap gin was more popular than beer—pictures such as Hogarth's *Gin Lane* visibly illustrate the consequences.

A law passed in 1743 that went into effect in 1751 raised the taxes on alcohol sales, allowing for controls on the sale of gin. These measures resulted in an improvement not only in the quality of gin but in the distillers' reputations as well.

In 1830 Aeneas Coffey introduced his continuous still, which produced a purer alcohol that could be redistilled with herbs and spices. Thus was created the lighter, purer alcohol that forms the basis of the unsweetened, subtly aromatic gin known as London dry gin.

Quality gin, as we know it today, was first made at the beginning of this century.

TYPES OF GIN

Dry gin—unsweetened gin
London dry gin—unsweetened gin
Old Tom gin—slightly sweetened gin
Plym or **Plymouth gin**—slightly sweetened gin

Gin compounds are not terribly popular. In a gin compound the gin absorbs the color and the aroma of the ingredient it is mixed with.

Sloe gin—mixed with blackthorn plum

Almond gin—mixed with bitter almond

Apple gin—mixed with apple

Lemon gin—mixed with lemon and/or lemon peel extract

Orange gin—mixed with bitter orange

Black currant gin—mixed with black currant

GERMAN GIN—The juniper schnapps **Steinhäger** is often called "German gin." Its flavor is indeed like gin, but Steinhäger is distilled from a fermented juniper berry mash. In contrast to gin, Steinhäger may not contain any additional aromatic ingredients (see Distillates from Fruit).

DUTCH GIN (Genever)—The national liquor of Holland is a full-flavored type of gin generally distilled from a **mix of grains** (1/3 barley, 1/3 rye, 1/3 corn). It was being distilled in Schiedam near Rotterdam as early as the end of the fifteenth century.

The flavor of Genever comes from the high proportion of **malted barley** used as the basis of distillation. This *moutwijn* (Dutch for malt wine) is triple distilled; in the third distillation aromatic ingredients such as juniper berries, anise, caraway, and so forth are added. In *Oude* (old) *Genever* (also spelled *Jenever*), this malt wine plays approximately the same role that malt whisky plays in a blended Scotch. It is the flavoring agent and is blended with grain alcohol. Oude Genever must contain a minimum of 5 percent *moutwijn;* in quality brands the percentage is significantly higher.

Jonge (young) *Genever*, by contrast, is a much simpler, less aromatic clear liquor that is made with little or even no *moutwijn*. Other countries also produce Genever-style gins, but only in Holland is the use of *moutwijn* a requirement.

The most famous Dutch brands:
Bokma
De Kuyper

Some well-known brands of gin are:

Beefeater–London distilled dry gin, the third most popular in the world (the only gin that is made with water from London), England, 94° proof

Bombay–London dry gin, England, 80° proof; Sapphire, 94° proof

Booth's–High & Dry, England, 80° proof; House of Lords (yellowish tone comes from cask storage), England, 86° proof

Fleischmann's–dry gin, United States, 80° proof

Gilbey's–London dry gin, the second most popular in the world (over 50 million bottles sold annually), England, 80–90° proof

Gordon's–London dry gin, the most popular in the world (over 100 million bottles sold in over 100 countries annually), England, 76° proof

Tanqueray–London dry gin, England, 86° proof

Pimm's No. 1–gin-based liquor, England, 66° proof

GIN AT THE BAR A bar without gin is like an Italian kitchen without pasta. Gin at the bar is as fundamental as spaghetti al pomodoro is in an Italian restaurant: it provides the base for an endless variety of famous concoctions that can be created wherever a skilled bartender is at work. No other liquor provides for the creation of so many classic cocktails.

Without gin the king of cocktails, the dry Martini, wouldn't exist; nor would the most popular alcoholic thirst quencher, the Gin & Tonic, nor the Pink Gin, the "medicine" of the bar.

The most famous highball of all would also not exist—the Gin Fizz, which was consumed during Prohibition. And of course Philip Marlowe's favorite drink, the Gimlet, would not exist.

To me, gin is the most fundamental liquor for mixed drinks. If I had to choose just one liquor, it would most certainly be gin. Gin is patient, it is aromatic, delicate, and unobtrusive, and thus is ideal for mixed drinks more than any other alcohol. It requires no additional liquor to enhance it. **Gin is a liquor that is harmonious with almost everything.** As a matter of respect I never mix it with any other base alcohol.

Gin and vodka together are unthinkable for me. Gin with brandy, whisk(e)y, tequila, or rum—why would one mix these? Gin and liqueurs—a natural. Gin and juices, gin and vermouth, gin and bitters—perfect!

AQUAVIT

Aquavit (*aqua vitae,* or water of life) is a spirit whose flavor comes from many spices, but the predominant spice is either caraway or dill. The basis of aquavit is a highly rectified, very pure agricultural (grain or potato) alcohol that is 192° proof and almost neutral in taste. This is distilled together with water, caraway, and a blend of spices that varies from brand to brand (generally including coriander, fennel, cinnamon, clove, and dill, among others). The combination and the exact blend of spices is essentially what distinguishes one brand from another.

The "heart" (middle runnings) of the distillation, separated from the first and last runnings, is known as the spice distillate and is mixed in an aquavit tank to the desired concentration with neutral alcohol and distilled or demineralized water and then stored to mature. The premium brands are aged in wooden casks, occasionally even in sherry casks.

Aquavit is the liquor of Scandinavia. It is produced mainly in Denmark, Norway, Sweden, and Finland.

A few famous brands are:

Aalborg Akvavit–light, clear grain spirit, caraway bouquet, Denmark, 84° proof

Aalborg Jubiläums Akvavit–golden yellow, caraway-dill bouquet, particularly mild, Denmark, 84° proof

Linie Aquavit–aquavit that is stored in sherry casks aboard ships and that crosses the equator twice during the aging process, Norway, 83° proof

Bommerlunder–the number-one German brand of aquavit, with a hint of anise, Germany, 76° proof

Malteserkreuz–produced in Germany according to an original Danish recipe, delicately spiced, 80° proof

WHISK(E)Y

Both whisky (the Scottish and Canadian spelling) and whiskey (the Irish and American spelling) are grain-based alcohols. The difference between the types of whisk(e)ys from the four main countries that produce it—Scotland, Ireland, the United States, and Canada—results from the kind of grain used and how it is processed, different methods of distillation, and different aging methods, not to mention the different kinds of blends.

SCOTCH WHISKY

Single malt—unblended 100 percent malt whisky, aged a minimum of three years, from a single distillery

Vatted malt—also known as pure malt or all malt; made of different single malts from different distilleries

Blended Scotch—malt whisky blended with grain whisky. A standard blend consists of thirty to forty different whiskies—both malt and grain—of which the portion of malt whisky can vary between 5 and 70 percent. Blended Scotch with a high proportion of malt whisky is referred to as a "deluxe blend."

SINGLE MALT WHISKY

Malt whisky in Scotland is made exclusively from malted barley, which means that prior to distillation the grain is softened in water, germinated, and eventually dried over peat in a kiln. One of the elements that typifies malt whisky is the smoky flavor that

comes from the peat in the kiln over which the germinated barley is dried. The goal of this entire process is to release the strong malt sugars from the barley so that they can eventually ferment. The malt is heated with water and mixed with yeast. The liquid strained after the two-day fermenting process is a

brew ("wash") containing about 5–8 percent alcohol by volume that is not unlike beer.

Also contributing to the unmistakable aroma of malt whisky is the water used in the malt and brewing, which in Scotland is generally soft and very rich in minerals. Every distillery greatly values the quality of its own well waters.

For malt whisky the fermented wash must be double distilled. The centuries-old, time-consuming, and labor-intensive "pot-still" method is employed for the production of malt whisky. Pot stills are onion-shaped copper kettles in which the wash is distilled and in which the vapors of the liquor are condensed in spiral tubes surrounded by cold water. The form and size of this apparatus determines the specific results of the distillation and accounts for subtle differences in flavor of various malts. The "low wines" obtained from the first distillation contain about 28 percent alcohol by volume. The second distillation takes place in a smaller pot still; at this stage it is important to ensure that the middle runnings are carefully separated, because this distillate is of most desirable quality. The first runnings and last runnings ("feints") contain impurities and will be redistilled another time. Determining which part of the distillate meets proper standards, that is, what constitutes the middle runnings, is the main responsibility and the art of the distiller.

The fresh spirit ("baby whisky") is colorless and contains just under 70 percent alcohol by volume; it is diluted with well water to about 63 percent alcohol by volume and then aged for several years in oak casks. The duration of aging and type of cask is of great significance in the maturation process. Gener-

ally American Bourbon casks are used (in the United States these casks may be used one time only for aging Bourbon), but some distillers emphasize that aging in sherry casks is what creates the distinctive character of their products.

A cask's origin, size, and permeability to air is what finally determines the color and aroma of a whisky. The minimum legal aging period is three years, but malt whisky is normally aged for eight to twelve years. Some malts reach their peak after ten years, but others are not finished until twenty-one to twenty-five years' aging. Very few malts—premium products that only collectors are prepared to buy—can be aged longer. As a rule, aging beyond fifteen years does not further improve quality; rather the whisky begins to dry out, absorbing excess flavor from the wood cask. After it has aged, the whisky is bottled, although some independent distilleries offer it in its original form and in cask strength. Most dilute their products with well water to a consumable strength (80–86° proof) and filter out the various sediments—which always contain more or less aromatic substances—by means of a special process (cold filtering). To ensure that the flavor of a particular whisky remains unchanged over years—that is, in order to create a brand—most producers mix in a certain ratio of different whisky vintages. As long as the individual whiskies are from the same distillery, the blend may still be sold as "single malt." If, however, malts from different distilleries are "married," the product is called "vatted malt." Incidentally, there are also some brands on the market that are sold exclusively as "pure malt," although "pure" may be synonymous with "vatted."

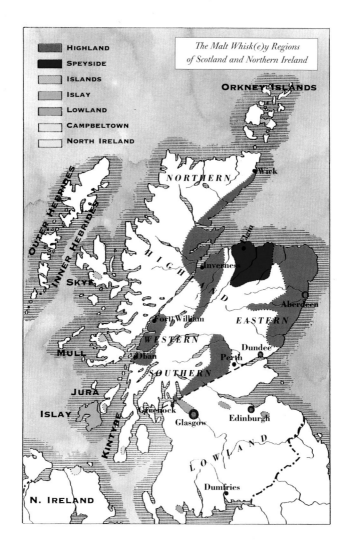

HIGHLAND
SPEYSIDE
ISLANDS
ISLAY
LOWLAND
CAMPBELTOWN
NORTH IRELAND

*The Malt Whisk(e)y Regions
of Scotland and Northern Ireland*

ORKNEY ISLANDS

OUTER HEBRIDES

INNER HEBRIDES

NORTHERN

Wick

HIGHLAND

Skye

SKYE

Inverness

Aberdeen

EASTERN

Fort William

WESTERN

MULL

Oban

Dundee

Perth

SOUTHERN

JURA

ISLAY

Greenock

Glasgow

Edinburgh

KINTYRE

LOWLAND

N. IRELAND

Dumfries

The hundred or so malt distilleries are separated into different groups by their geographical location. Although distinct differences in flavor exist between some regions, this classification is geographical and by no means should be taken as an automatic indication about particular flavors.

HIGHLANDS All malts that are produced north of a border between Greenock in the west and Dundee in the east are called Highland malts. There are yet more geographical subdivisions within this area, but only Speyside malts can be called a truly autonomous group. The center of malt production lies along the Spey River. Every few kilometers there is a distillery; among them are **Glenfiddich**, **Glenlivet**, and **Knockando**, the leading brands on the market. The large companies **Macallan** and **Glenfarclas** also make their home here.

There is no consistent Highlands taste. Exquisite Cognac-like brands such as **Dalmore** and **Macallan** are produced here, as are the mild **Oban** and **Knockando** and the rich **Clynelish** and **Linkwood**. A further distinction in addition to the Highlands of the Speyside area can be made between the northern, western, and eastern Highlands. Malts from the Orkney Islands, Jura, or Skye are often grouped as Highland malts.

LOWLANDS South of the border between Greenock and Dundee lie the Lowland distilleries. The lightest malts, well suited as aperitifs, come from this area, such as **Rosebank** and **Auchentoshan**, both of which are **triple distilled**.

CAMPBELTOWN Once the capital city of whisky in Scotland, this town in Mull of Kintyre today distributes only the individualistic **Springbank Malt**

ISLAY The island of Islay markets the strongest-flavored of all malts. Peaty water lends the whisky a strong pungency, occasionally nearly medicinal. Prized among connoisseurs, the most important of these malts are **Lagavulin**, **Bowmore**, and **Laphroaig**

SKYE From this island comes the exceptional **Talisker**, which combines the richness of Islay malts with the delicacy of Highland malts.

JURA, MULL, ORKNEY The somewhat different whiskies of these three islands share the flavor characteristics of Highland malts.

IRELAND Bushmills, the only Irish malt, has been produced since 1608 in the town of Bushmills in the northern Irish county of Antrim.

Although malt is indisputedly the best of all whiskies, only an infinitesimally small portion of it is bottled. The vastly larger part is used in blends with grain whisky, to produce blended Scotch.

An assortment of malts:

Aberlour (Speyside), 12 years old, 86° proof

Ardbeg (Islay), 10 years old, 80° proof; 15 years old, 91° proof

Auchentoshan (Lowland), 10 years old, 80° proof

Aultmore (Speyside), 12 years old, 80° proof

The Balvenie (Speyside), 80° and 86° proof

Bowmore (Islay), 12 years old, 86° proof

Bruichladdich (Islay), 10 years old, 80° proof

Bunnahabhain (Islay), 12 years old, 86° proof

Cardhu (Speyside), 12 years old, 80° proof

Clynelish (Highland), 12 years old, 114° proof

Cragganmore (Speyside), 12 years old, 80° proof

Dalmore (Highland), 12 years old, 80° proof

Dalwhinnie (Highland), 15 years old, 86° proof

Glendronach (Speyside), 12 years old, 80° and 86° proof

Glenfarclas (Speyside), 8–25 years old, 80°, 86°, 92°, 120° proof

Glenfiddich (Speyside), 80° proof

Glen Grant (Speyside), 10–25 years old, 80°, 86°, and 92° proof

The Glenlivet (Speyside), 12 years old, 86° proof

Glenmorangie (Highland), 10 years old, 80° proof

Highland Park (Orkney), 12 years old, 80° proof

Isle of Jura (Isle of Jura), 8 years old, 80° proof

Knockando (Speyside), vintage whisky, 86° proof

Lagavulin (Islay), 16 years old, 86° proof

Laphroaig (Islay), 10 years old, 86° proof

Linkwood (Speyside), 15 years old, 80° proof

Lochnagar (Highland), 12 years old, 86° proof

Longmorn (Speyside), 12 years old, 86° proof; 25 years old, 86° proof

The Macallan (Speyside), 12 years old, 86° proof; 25 years old, 86° proof

Mortlach (Speyside), 12 years old, 80° proof

Oban (Highland), 12 years old, 86° proof; 14 years old, 86° proof

Rosebank (Lowland), 8 years old, 80° proof

Scapa (Orkney), 8 years old, 80° proof

The Singleton (Speyside), vintage bottles, 80° proof

Springbank (Campbeltown), 12–30 years old, 92° proof

Strathisla (Speyside), 15 years old, 80° proof

Talisker (Skye), 8 years old, 91.6° proof

Tamdhu (Speyside), 10 years old, 80° proof

Tamnavulin (Speyside), 10 years old, 80° proof

Tormore (Speyside), 10 years old, 80° proof

GRAIN WHISKY

Grain whisky is distilled from unmalted grains, primarily corn, and to a smaller extent malted barley. The distilling does not, however, take place in a pot still, but in a continuous still, which makes efficient industrial production possible.

The grain is boiled in water under pressure, combined with yeast, and eventually transferred to enormous fermenting tanks. The distillation occurs in a so-called patent or Coffey still, which consists of two tall connected copper tubes in which steam and the mash are continually and simultaneously channeled. A complicated system of ventilation and separators inside the still ensures that after a relatively brief time very

pure alcohol can be obtained (rectification). The result is a lighter, colorless, and nearly neutral-tasting grain alcohol.

Often it is said that grain whisky is not aged. But the vast majority of grain whiskies that will be combined with malt whiskies to make blended Scotch must indeed be aged, because the legal minimum for aging every single Scottish whisky applies not only to malt but to grain as well. The age listed on a blended Scotch, which always refers to the youngest individual distillate in the blend, includes grain whisky.

BLENDED SCOTCH

Scottish whisky first earned its worldwide reputation in a blended form probably because the addition of the light-bodied grain to the malt whisky reduced the intensity and broadened its appeal.

A blend may contain between fifteen and fifty different malt whiskies of various characters and ages, in addition to two or three grain whiskies. Every firm tries to achieve the most consistent product possible. Because most blends consist mostly of colorless grain whisky, a sweet coloring agent (caramel) is added to achieve a genuine whisky color. The quality of a blend depends on the portion of malt it contains (5–70 percent) and its age (when it contains more than a certain portion of old—and thus expensive—malt, it is called a "deluxe blend"). Also significant is whether the final product is aged in oak casks for a few months prior to being bottled or is bottled directly after it is assembled—which of course is less expensive. In any case even the most attractive and expensive "deluxe blend" can't hold a candle to a pure malt.

Some famous brands:

The Antiquary Deluxe, 12 years old, 80° proof

Ballantine's Finest Scotch, 80° proof; 12, 17, 30 years old, 86° proof

Bell's Extra Special, 12 years old, 86° proof; Deluxe, 20 years old, 86° proof; Royal Reserve, 30 years old, 86° proof (many special bottlings)

Black & White, 80° proof

Buchanan's Reserve, 12 years old, 86° proof

Chivas Regal, 12 years old, 86° proof; Royal Salute, 86° proof

Clan Campbell, 5, 12 years old, 86° proof; Deluxe, 12 years old, 80° proof

Cutty Sark 12 years old, 86° proof

Dewar's White Label, 12 years old, 80° proof

Dimple Haig, 12 years old, 80° proof

Famous Grouse (the grouse is the Scottish national symbol), 80° proof

Grant's, 12 years old, 80° proof

Haig Gold Label, 86° proof

Highland Queen, 86° proof; Grand Reserve, 15 years old, 86° proof

J & B (Justerini & Brooks), 86° proof

Johnnie Walker Red Label, 86° proof; Black Label, 12 years old, 80° proof; Swing, 12 years old, 86° proof

King Georg IV, 80° proof

King's Ransom, 12 years old, 86° proof

Logan Deluxe, 80° proof

Long John Deluxe, 80° and 86° proof

Old Parr Deluxe, 12 years old, 86° proof

Teacher's Highland Cream, 80° proof

Usher's, 80° proof

Vat 69, 86° proof

White Horse, 80° proof

Whyte & Mackay, 80° proof

IRISH WHISKEY

Grain distillation is a process known in Ireland for centuries, and the Irish claim that the Emerald Isle can be considered the true cradle of all whisk(e)y. Today, four out of the five main brands of Irish whiskey are produced in the central distillery in Midleton in Cork County. Irish distillers built this large facility when they consolidated into a group, which has since come under the ownership of Pernod-Ricard. Also belonging to this association is the Bushmills distillery in the northern Irish county of Antrim. It, however, distills only its own products.

Despite the centralization, every Irish whiskey remains, as ever, an individual product. In Midleton every brand is produced according to its original recipe. The original Irish whiskey is made in pot stills, but since the last century malted barley is not used alone, nor is it distilled only in pot stills, but also in column stills. For Irish whiskey the barley is not kiln dried over peat, and thus lacks the smoky aroma typical of Scotch.

For every whiskey the individual grain types are distilled by different methods, and they are used in varying quantities. The distillers use pot and patent stills (column stills) in custom-made sequences for each brand: pot-patent-pot, for example, for one, pot-pot-patent, for another. Malt whiskeys are a component of Irish whiskey, as are light-bodied grain whiskeys. The very different distillates are individually aged for every brand.

One of the special features of Irish whiskey is that its flavor from cask aging is much stronger than Scottish or American brands. About 5 percent of the casks used for Irish whiskey formerly held sherry; some were once filled with rum, and the rest are used Bourbon casks. Because the casks play such an important role, what is known as blending in Scotland is instead known in Ireland as vatting.

The most important brands:

Bushmills Black Bush, 80° proof; Old Bushmills, 80° and 86° proof; Malt, 10 years old, 80° proof

John Jameson, 80° proof; 12 years old, 86° proof

Midleton Very Rare, 80° proof

Paddy, 80° proof

Power's, 80° proof

Tullamore Dew, 80° proof

AMERICAN WHISKEY

American whiskey falls into three broad categories:

Straight whiskeys—the unblended product of a distillation from at least 51 percent of a single grain. Examples include Bourbon (from corn) and rye (from rye)

Blended whiskeys—must contain a minimum of 20 percent straight whiskey, blended with a neutral grain spirit or light whiskey

Light whiskeys—these whiskeys have less flavor intensity than straight whiskeys and are used primarily for blending

BOURBON is the most well known of the various kinds of whiskey produced in the United States. The term *Bourbon* reflects its place of origin (Bourbon County, Kentucky), but actually refers only to a special production method—not a geographical appellation. In Bourbon County these days there is no longer any whiskey production.

Bourbon is made from at least 51 percent corn, which is fermented with malted grain and yeast added and is eventually distilled by a method similar to the patent or continuous still method (as in grain whisky production). The fermentation is usually carried out according to the "sour mash" method, which means that the liquid to be fermented is combined with the yeast-containing residue from the previous distillation. This brings about not only an intensification of the (sweet) flavor, but also ensures that the character of the whiskey remains consistent from distillation to distillation. After distillation, the whiskey must be reduced to 125° proof by adding water, and it must be aged for a minimum of two years in new oak casks that have been charred inside, which accelerates the coloration of the whiskey. (In practice, most Bourbons are aged four years or more.) The subtle sweetness and the underlying vanilla bouquet of Bourbon are to a large extent the result of the specially treated new oak cask the Bourbon is aged in.

In recent years, single-barrel and small-batch Bourbons—essentially limited-production, well-aged, high-quality straight whiskeys—have been marketed. Often aged six to ten years, these whiskeys are much smoother and more complex than typical Bourbons. Among them are **Knob Creek**, **Booker's**, and **Hancock's**.

Famous Bourbons are: **Ancient Age**, **Maker's Mark**, **Wild Turkey**, **Jim Beam**, **Old Grand-Dad**, and **Old Crow**.

TENNESSEE The sour mash whiskeys produced in Tennessee do not differ significantly from Bourbon in their production but rather in their notable smoothness. This is the result of a special filtration process that takes place after the whiskey is cask aged. The whiskey trickles through layers

of charcoal several yards thick to strain out the remaining flavor impurities. Classic examples are **Jack Daniels** and **George Dickel**.

RYE WHISKEY Rye whiskey is an American invention. This drink, popular until the 1950s, is produced today by a process comparable to Bourbon; however, rye is somewhat more pungent than Bourbon. Rye must contain at least 51 percent rye and is generally aged for four years (it is not, as many people assume, a blended whiskey). A good example is **Old Overholt.**

An assortment of American whiskeys:

Ancient Age—Kentucky Straight Bourbon, 86° proof

George Dickel—Tennessee Sour Mash, 86° proof

Four Roses—Straight Bourbon, 80° proof

I. W. Harper—Kentucky Straight Bourbon, 80° proof

Jack Daniels—Tennessee Sour Mash, 86° proof; Green Label, 86° proof available only in the United States

Jim Beam—Kentucky Straight Bourbon, Sour Mash, 80° and 90° proof (Black Label)

Old Crow—Kentucky Straight Bourbon, Sour Mash, 80° proof

Old Fitzgerald—Kentucky Straight Bourbon, Sour Mash, 86° and 90° proof; Very Old

Fitzgerald, 8 years old, 100° proof; Very Very Old Fitzgerald, 12 and 15 years old, 100° proof

Old Forester—Kentucky Straight Bourbon, Sour Mash, 86° and 100° proof

Old Grand-Dad—Kentucky Straight Bourbon, 80° proof; 114 Barrel Proof, 114° proof; 10 years old, 114° proof

Old Overholt—Straight Rye Whiskey, 86° proof

Old Weller—Kentucky Straight Bourbon, 107° proof

Seagram's 7 Crown—American Blended Whiskey, 80° proof

Walker's Deluxe—Kentucky Straight Bourbon, 6 years old, 80° proof

Wild Turkey—Kentucky Straight Bourbon, 101° proof

CANADIAN WHISKY

Canadian whisky was traditionally based on rye, but there is no pure rye Canadian whisky that is comparable to a straight rye from the United States. Of course a pure rye distillate is matured in Canada's distilleries, as is a pure distillate from corn, from malted and unmalted barley, and from other grains—but these are used for blending, which is common to all Canadian whiskies. In making their blends, every producer makes distillates from different raw materials and by different processes. Canadians primarily use the continual still, but it is much more versatile there than elsewhere. As in Ireland, different types of distilling apparatuses are used in combination with each other. The goal is always to obtain a distillate that is as pure as possible, and it must be double distilled. The numerous different individual whiskies are aged separately, either in new casks or in sherry, Bourbon, or brandy casks. Three years is the minimum aging period permitted, but on average the whiskies are aged four to six years. Canadian whiskies are always blends of individual whiskies with varying characteristics and an almost neutral alcohol (which in special cases may also be distilled from rye). Some manufacturers make blends prior to cask aging; others do not mix them until the individual whiskies have matured. The high portion (often over 90 percent by volume) of neutral alcohol and the comparatively high-grade distilled individual whiskies used allow for only small differences to exist between different brands—

Canadian whisky is light-bodied and not as rich or expressive as other whisk(e)ys.

The most famous brands:

Black Velvet, 80° proof
Canadian Club, 80° proof; Classic, 12 years old, 80° proof
Schenley O.F.C. (Old Fine Canadian), 8 years old, 80° proof
Seagram's V.O., 6 years old, 86° proof; Crown Royal, 80° proof
Windsor Supreme, 80° proof
McGuiness, 8 years old, 80° proof

WHISK(E)Y AT THE BAR In principle malt whisky ought not to be diluted. If served on the rocks, the ice will not only water it down, but will also chill it too greatly, because its character only fully unfolds at a temperature of 68°F. It is advisable to add a few drops of water (never soda water) to smoky whiskies containing a high percentage of malt; this accentuates the fullness of all the nuances of flavor in the whisky. In Scotland there are small "nosing glasses," which are similar to sherry copitas and particularly well suited to capture the bouquet of a malt. Large Cognac snifters (though not too large) also achieve this effect, whereas normal whiskey tumblers are unsuitable for malts. It is customary to serve a glass of (ice) water on the side, because whisky is not a thirst-quenching drink. In contrast to clear liquors, it should be enjoyed in small, languorous sips. This enhances not only its flavor but also its digestibility.

Over time a custom of serving malt whisky not only before and after dinner but occasionally also with dinner in place of wine has developed in Scotland, in which case the rule of thumb is: the heavier the dish, the more flavorful the whisky.

Whereas Irish whiskey is either diluted 1:1 with water or, like malt, is served neat, blended Scotch and American whisk(e)ys are served on the rocks. Scotch may also be combined with lemon mixers, and American whiskey is the classic base in cocktails.

MYSTIQUE No liquor is held in such reverence as whisk(e)y. Once one has experienced fine whisk(e)y, one will tolerate no spirits above it!

Whisk(e)y drinkers remain loyal to their type of whisk(e)y and often even to a particular brand. They drink it neat—without ice, with a water chaser.

Some whisk(e)y cocktails are bar classics, such as the **Manhattan**, **Old-Fashioned**, and **Whiskey Sour**. They are mixed with Bourbon, but they may also be made with Canadian or Scotch whisky.

VODKA

According to one definition, vodka is a spirit "that is derived from ethyl alcohol of agricultural origin, either by rectification or filtration through charcoal—and if necessary, is subsequently singly distilled—or by a similar process, which selectively attenuates the characteristics of the basic material used." Obviously, then, vodka does not have to be made strictly from grain; potatoes, for example, serve just as well as a basis for its alcohol. But it is true that premium brands are almost always distilled from grain, primarily from barley and wheat, and occasionally from rye. Some of these brands carry the description "grain vodka."

Russia and Poland are still considered the classic native lands of vodka, but the United States, the largest marketer of vodka in the world, has meanwhile taken the lead in production: Smirnoff, produced worldwide in thirty-three facilities under American supervision, is the number-one vodka and second only to Bacardi rum in international sales. But vodkas from Scandinavia (Sweden, Finland), and the German vodka Gorbatschow have also become market leaders. Distillation rather than rectification (purification) is the method more often employed to produce a mild, pure vodka of a nearly neutral flavor. Far more important than the distillation itself are the different techniques of filtration, which result in a particularly pure distillate. Today the charcoal filtration method is generally preferred, producing clear, clean vodka. Small amounts of lightly aromatic substances are permitted as additives in vodka. Vodkas containing buffalo grass are among the most well known aromatic vodkas. Other brands are flavored with pepper, sherry, or lemon.

Most famous vodkas:

Absolut—Sweden, 80° proof

Gorbatschow—Germany, 80° proof

Grasovka (flavored with buffalo grass)—Poland, 80° proof

Finlandia—Finland, 95° proof

Krepkaya (strong)—Russia/Poland, 110° proof

Moskovskaya—Russia, 80° proof

Smirnoff—United States (for Germany, manufactured in France), 80° proof; Blue Label, 100° proof

Stolichnaya (table vodka)—Russia, 80° proof

Wyborowa—Poland, 80° proof

Zubrowka (flavored with bison grass)—Russia, 80° proof

VODKA AT THE BAR As a mixer, vodka is always overshadowed by its "brother" gin, even though its neutral flavor makes it ideal for mixed drinks. There are nonetheless a multitude of famous, classic cocktails that are vodka based, for example, the **Bloody Mary**, **Harvey Wallbanger**, and **Screwdriver**.

Vodka is the winner of "straight ups" at the bar the world over. In the past and still today drinkers who prefer their liquor straight up agree that vodka is the spirit least likely to give one a hangover.

DISTILLATES FROM FRUIT

Within the general category of fruit brandies, a distinction is made between distillates from **pomaceous fruits** (apples and pears), **stone fruits** (cherries, plums, etc.), and **berries** (raspberries, blackberries, etc.). According to European Community regulations, fruit brandies and such made from fruit skins and husks must be a minimum of 75° proof. Quality fruit brandies are never less than 80° proof and are often stronger.

Fruit brandies produced from the skins and husks of pomaceous and stone fruits, primarily in France, cannot be compared to "genuine" fruit brandies such as kirschwasser, poire Williams, and eau-de-vie de framboise. Further, there is a difference between fruit spirits and fruit waters.

DISTILLATION Although fruit brandies can be distilled from fermented fruit mash (such as apples), other fruits can be macerated with neutral spirits and then redistilled. This enables spirits to be produced from sugar-poor (and thus not capable of fermentation) fruits—that is, berry-type fruits such as raspberries, blackberries, and currants.

AGING Fruit-distilled wines are aged in clay, stone, or glass containers. This keeps them colorless and clear, whereas the exceptions that are cask aged will turn yellowish. Only Calvados is sometimes of a brown tone.

DISTILLATES FROM POMACEOUS FRUITS

The best-known pomaceous fruit distillates are made from apple and pear. At the top of the list is **Calvados**, although it isn't strictly comparable to the standard fruit brandies extracted directly from the fruit.

Calvados is produced in Normandy. Connoisseurs look for bottlings from the eleven defined areas of production (Appellations d'Origine Contrôlée), of which Pays d'Auge is considered the best.

PRODUCTION The basic material is apple must, or **cider** (*cidre*), in which a total of forty-eight kinds of apple may be used. Quality-conscious distillers age the cider for some weeks, often even longer, before it is distilled, because the aging process results in more delicate aromatic substances in the distillation. Calvados from Pays d'Auge must be double distilled by the pot-still method; those from the other ten regions are usually distilled by the continuous-still method.

In the traditional double-distillation process the coarse brandy rests for some months in oak or chestnut casks before the second distillation. Whether double or continuous distilled, the fresh distillate is still raw and very high in alcoholic content. Cask aging and later reducing the strength with processed water is what creates an aromatic Calvados out of strong brandy.

Some descriptions on labels about the minimal period of cask aging:

2 years: 3 stars or 3 apples
3 years: Calvados Vieux or Réserve
4 years: V.O., Vieille Réserve
5 years: V.S.O.P.
older: Hors d'Age, Extra, Napoléon, Age Inconnu

Marc de pommes is made from the peels and residual apple.

Apple brandies that do not come from Calvados are called eau-de-vie de pomme, apple brandy, or applejack (United States), and aguardiente di sidre (Spain, aged in sherry casks).

OTHER DISTILLATES FROM POMACEOUS FRUITS Among the most popular of this type of spirit is pear brandy, also known as **poire Williams**. The most famous product of this type is 86° proof Williamine, manufactured by the Swiss distillery Morand in Wallis.

BRANDY WINE FROM STONE FRUITS

The most important stone-fruit brandy is kirschwasser, such as **Schwarzwälder kirsch**, **eau-de-vie de cerises** (sweet cherries), or **eau-de-vie de girottes** (sour cherries). Distillers consider kirsch to be the most difficult fruit brandy to produce. There is a large assortment of cherry types that are suitable for distilling; the best are small, sweet mountain-grown cherries that are, however, not very fleshy. The distiller must be careful that no stems are distilled with the cherries, that no spoiled cherries end up in the mash, and that the cherries are fully ripe but not fermenting. Kirschwasser is unforgiving of any mistakes. A little "hint of stone" (also "hint of wood") from the seeds can lend a kirsch a special nuance, but adding too much is a grave mistake. Like all liquors classified as waters, kirsch is made by distilling the alcohol that arises from the fermentation of the mash (double distillation, although a single-distillation process is also used with intensifiers added).

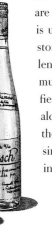

Other eaux-de-vie of significance are those made from plums (**quetsch**, **slivovitz**, and **eau-de-vie de prunes**). Delicious too are the waters going by the name

mirabelle made from the aromatic plum of the same name. Less significant, but worth a try, are the fruit brandies of **quince** (*coing*) and the very popular **apricot brandies** known in Austria as Marillen brandy and in Hungary as Barack Pálinka.

BRANDY WINE FROM BERRIES

Brandies made from berries are distilled as "spirits." These fruits have too little sugar to ferment properly. The fruits are macerated, that is, they are soaked in neutral agricultural alcohol, which absorbs the flavors. The alcohol is subsequently distilled together with the berries. Generally, such spirits are at least 80° proof, but most are stronger; some are even up to 90° proof.

The most famous berry brandy is **raspberry spirit** (eau-de-vie de framboise). Other berry spirits are made from **bilberries**, **blackberries**, **strawberries** (*fraise*), **black** and **red currant** (cassis, *groseille*), and **cranberries**.

Among berry brandies, **Steinhäger** is special. This juniper berry brandy, known in Westphalia since the sixteenth century, is distilled from previously fermented juniper berries.

Some liqueurs are also produced using these brandies as a base, most of which are crèmes, such as crème de cassis.

In contrast to berry spirits, these liqueurs are frequently used in bars—most are mixed with a small amount of wine or sparkling wine (for example, **Kir** and **Kir Royal**).

FRUIT BRANDIES AT THE BAR The classic fruit brandies—which German and Swiss firms have the longest tradition of manufacturing—do not play a terribly significant role in creating mixed drinks at the bar.

By contrast, the recently created **tropical fruit spirits**, made, for example, of banana, mandarin, mango, maracuja (passion fruit), and papaya, are excellent in mixed drinks with syrups and nectars of the same fruits. As an **aperitif**, restaurants serve, among others, an ounce of exotic-fruit brandies in a Champagne flute. Gourmets particularly enjoy kirschwasser, poire Williams, and exotic-fruit brandies neat as digestifs. A poll has shown that fruit brandies—even more than Cognac—are the most popular after-dinner drinks.

Fruit brandies served neat should not be chilled! Connoisseurs prefer them served at about 65°F in a chilled "nosing glass" to enjoy fully their taste and bouquet.

DISTILLATES FROM PLANTS

RUM

Ron (Spanish/Portuguese), Rhum (French), Rum (English/German)

Rum is one of the oldest liquors in the world, dating from the seventeenth century. It can be nearly colorless, light-bodied, and faintly aromatic, or dark brown, richly aromatic, flavorful, and heavy-bodied.

THE MOST SIGNIFICANT COUNTRIES OF ORIGIN

Greater Antilles (Cuba, Jamaica, Haiti, Puerto Rico, and the Dominican Republic); **Lesser Antilles** (such as the Virgin Islands, Martinique, Guadeloupe, Trinidad, and Barbados); **South America**: British Guyana (Demerara), Dutch Guyana (Surinam), French Guyana (Cayenne), Brazil, and Venezuela. In addition: the **United States, Mexico, Philippines**, Madagascar, Réunion.

PRODUCTION To rum connoisseurs, the place and method of distillation is of great importance—**rum experts differentiate between as many rum flavors as wine experts do with wines.** The fundamental basis of all types of rum is the sticky, brown molasses residue that remains when the sugar is boiled down (the exception is rum that is made only of sugar cane juice or sugar cane syrup). Sugar cane, which grows as high as twenty feet, has a pulp that consists of up to 90 percent sweet juice, which is as much as 18 percent sugar. The residual molasses is still rich in sugar that does not crystallize in the process of separating the sugar and molasses. It is in fact so rich that it cannot begin to ferment until it is diluted with water. Before the fermentation "skimming" and "dunder" may be added to the diluted molasses. "Skimming" is the foam that rises to the surface when the sugar cane juice is strained, and "dunder" is a nonalcoholic residue of yeast, bacteria, and acids that remains in the still from an earlier distillation. Both are crucial to the flavor and aroma of rum.

Some kinds of rum, such as French rum from Martinique, are distilled directly from pure sugar cane juice or sugar cane syrup. Economically more efficient and widespread, however, was and is the practice that allows the sugar cane juice to serve two purposes: the sugar is separated in one facility, and the rum is distilled from the residual substances in a rum manufacturing facility next door. Because of dwindling international prospects for marketing sugar cane, the customary arrangement of a sugar manufacturer and a rum manufacturer side by side has become less common.

Exactly which aromatic cultures and which kind of yeast and bacteria cultures each rum manufacturer adds to the mash of molasses, water, skimming, and dunder when he sets the fermentation process in motion remains a secret. In rum manufacturing this process is normally extremely turbulent and reaches its peak after only twenty or thirty hours. But by controlling the surrounding temperature it is prolonged for some types of rum by as much as twelve days. **Slow fermentation results in a stronger bouquet.** The additional enzymes split the sugar in the alcohol and the carbon dioxide, a process that causes the mash to begin to simmer and boil in the vat, ending when the yeast cells, which have consumed all the sugar, die off. In the subsequent distillation, the mash is heated, transforming the alcohol into a vapor, and then back into liquid by cooling it down. The true art of the distiller is to control the temperature precisely so that the desirable aromatic substances volatilize with the alcohol, and the undesirable aldehyde or fusel oils do not. To intensify the bouquet of a rum and give it a "personal nuance," many distillers add a few ingredients in the distillation, such as cinnamon, vanilla, pineapple, raisins, cloverleaf or peach leaves, acacia rinds, or plum extract.

There are two different distillation processes that produce radically different qualities of rum. The traditional method uses the **pot still**, in which the desirable aroma-strengthening elements are not separated from the alcohol. The result is a rich, heavy-bodied rum. These flavorful rums are produced in Jamaica, Haiti, and elsewhere.

Light-bodied rums are produced by the **continuous-** or **patent-still** method, which consists of a number of column stills into which different distillates with different boiling points are collected. This allows for a better separation of the undesirable aromatic substances, although it also means many of the flavors typical of rum are negated in the process. The mixture of the distillates results in light-bodied rums, which have by far surpassed the heavier types in the marketplace.

After the distillation is complete, the rum is still raw and crude tasting; depending on the distillation method employed and the "house recipe," it is between 130° and 180° proof. Only after months or years of aging do the acids, esters, and alcohol bind together: a requirement for an ultimately fine-tasting rum. Whether rum is dark or white depends only on how it is aged. Most rum is aged in charred oak casks, which colors it yellowish or brownish; if it is aged in stainless steel tanks, it remains colorless. The color of dark rum is frequently enhanced with cooked sugar or caramel. The "master blender" makes the decision about the final color and strength; he is the "maestro de ron," who is responsible for always maintaining the same mixture for a brand. **Quality and flavor are very different depending on the production area.**

SOME TYPES OF RUM

Puerto Rican rums–light-bodied rums by the world's leading producer

Jamaican rums–heavy-bodied, pungent rums famous for their flavor

Demerara rum (Navy rum)–a collective description for very dark, aromatic rum from Guyana and the West Indies, sometimes bottled at very high proofs—including 151° (overproof rums)

Rum brands:

Admiral Rodney—St. Lucia

Alleyne Arthur's—Barbados

Aniversario Pampero Añejo—Venezuela

Appleton—Jamaica

Bacardi—among others, Puerto Rico (the best-selling liquor in the world)

Barbancourt—Haiti

Barrilito—Puerto Rico

Bermudez—Dominican Republic

Boca Chica—Puerto Rico

Bologne—Guadeloupe

Bourdon—Guadeloupe

Buccaneer—Montserrat

Cacique—Venezuela

Caldas Rum—Columbia

Calypso–Barbados

Captain Morgan–Jamaica

Caribbean Gold–Jamaica

Castillo–Puerto Rico

Champion–Haiti

Clément–Martinique

Cockspur–Barbados

Columbus–Jamaica

Corona White–Jamaica

Coruba–Jamaica

Courantin–Guyana

Courville–Martinique

Crassous de Medeuil–Martinique

Cruzan–U.S. Virgin Islands

Del Barrilito–Puerto Rico

Demerara–Guyana

Denros Bounty–St. Lucia

Depaz–Martinique

Dillon–Martinique

VIRGIN ISLANDS

CRUZAN, RUM

WEST INDIES RUM

Light in character – of fine flavour and made in compliance with the highest standard of excellence

DISTILLED AND BOTTLED BY
Cruzan Rum Distillery Co.
ST. CROIX, VIRGIN ISLANDS

Don Q–Puerto Rico

Duquesne–Martinique

First Rate–Jamaica

Flor de Cabana Blanco–Jamaica

Forgeron–Jamaica

Fort Ille–Guadeloupe

Goddard's–Barbados

Granada Gold–Puerto Rico

Hardy–Martinique

Havana Club–Cuba (largest rum distillery in the world)

J. Bailly–Martinique

John Canoe–Jamaica

Kairi–Trinidad

La Favorite–Martinique

La Mauny–Martinique

Lamb's–England

Lasserre–Guadeloupe

Lemon Hart–England

Longueteau–Guadeloupe

Macoucherie–Dominica

Maniba–Martinique

Marie Colas–Haiti

Mirande–French Guyana

Mount Gay–Barbados

Myers's–Jamaica ("The Planter's Punch Brand")

Nazon–Haiti

Negrita–Martinique

Neron–Guadeloupe

Old Holborn Navy Rum–England

Old Nick–Martinique

Old Oak–Trinidad

Palo Viejo–Puerto Rico

Parker's Cresta–Jamaica

Paso Fino–Puerto Rico

Pott–Germany

Prévot–French Guyana

Pusser's British Navy Rum–England

Red Cap–Dominica

Red Heart–Jamaica

River Antoine–Grenada

Robinson–Jamaica

Ron Bocoy–Puerto Rico

Ron Llave–Puerto Rico

Ron Matusalem–Puerto Rico

Ronrico–Puerto Rico

St. Etienne–Martinique

St. James–Martinique

Soca–Dominica

Tabanou–Guadeloupe

Tesserot–Haiti

Trois Rivières–Martinique

Viejo de Caldas–Columbia

White Cat Light & Dry–Aruba

CACHAÇA

Also known as caxaca, caxa, or chacha, the brandy made from sugar cane and Brazilian "ron" is—in contrast to white rum, which is usually obtained from molasses—**distilled directly from the juice of sugar cane**. Prior to the distillation, the juice ferments in a copper or wood container over three weeks and is then boiled down three times to a concentrate. According to brand, cachaça is either distilled by the pot still, like Cognac, or by the continuous-still method, but always in such a way that the scent of sugar cane and inimitable flavor typical of rum are retained.

In Brazil there are hundreds of cachaça producers, including Pitú, with its red Brazilian freshwater crab logo. A large exporter of cachaça is Fazenda Soledad in Nova Friburgo in the vicinity of Rio de Janeiro. From there comes Nêga Fulô in its characteristic one-liter bottles encased in woven rattan.

The **Caipirinha**, the "drink of farmers" (*caipira* means farmer), Brazil's famous drink made with cachaça, lime, and sugar, has made cachaça popular in many countries.

Famous brands:

Nêga Fulô—sugar cane brandy, Brazil, 86° proof
Pitú—sugar cane brandy, Brazil, 86° proof
Cachaça de Caricé—sugar cane brandy, Brazil, 86° proof

Cachaça Nêga Fulô

TEQUILA AND MEZCAL

The distilled spirits made from the agave plant.

PULQUE—fresh, fermented agave juice

TEQUILA—agave-distilled wine (from the blue-green Maguey agave) from a designated area in the Mexican state of Jalisco

MEZCAL—agave-distilled wine that does not come from the designated tequila area of Jalisco. Mezcal is only single distilled

TEQUILA PRODUCTION An albuminous juice called *aguamiel* (honey water) is obtained from the heart of agave plants ripe and ready for harvesting about ten years after planting. This fresh agave juice is then mixed with pre-viously fermented agave juice (*pulque*, which was consumed by the Aztecs), trig-gering a quick and strong fermentation (about two and a half days). This brew is subsequently double distilled, producing clear white tequila. Gold-to-Cognac-brown tequilas get their color from aging up to four years in oak casks. Because of the  rising demand for tequila (for export and otherwise), some tequila producers feel compelled to distill sugar cane juice along with the agave, which is not exactly beneficial to the character of tequila.

Well-known tequila and mezcal brands:

Almeca Gold

Arandas Oro; White

Baja Tequila

Beamero Gold

Crendain Extra; Ollitas

Don Emilio Gold; White

El Gran Matador Gold; White

Fonda Blanca White

Gavilan Hawk Especial; White

Gusano Rojo Mezcal

Herradura Anejo; Reposado Gold; Silver

José Cuervo Blanco; Especial; Centenario; 1800

Matador White

Miguel de la Mezcal

Monte Alban Mezcal

Montezuma Gold; White

Old Mr. Boston Golden

Olé Gold; White

Olmeca Gold

Pancho Villa Gold; White

Pepe Lopez de Oro; White

Sauza Commemorativo; Extra Gold; Hornitos; Silver

Sierra Tequila Silver; Gold; Antiguo

Tequila Espuela

Tequila Silla

Two Fingers Gold; Limitado; White

ARAK

Arak is a **collective term** for the vegetable distillate of the Orient known in Europe since the seventeenth century. The

raw material of arak is often **rice**, which is fermented, mixed with sugar (or molasses), and distilled. Arak may also be produced from **palms**, **dates**, **millet**, or **other plants**. Arak is especially widespread in the Far East (Java, Thailand, China); in Europe, Batavia-Arak from Java, among others, is known. It is distilled from rice and sugar cane molasses, often with a palm sap or rather palm wine (toddy) added to it. Its light golden color comes from a long period of aging in oak casks.

Arak has been almost entirely surpassed in the European market today by rum. But it is still used in the preparation of grog and of punches, although it may also be enjoyed neat.

Liqueurs

Liqueurs are sweetened liquors that are flavored and scented by the addition of spices, herbs, flowers, and so on.

The basis of all liqueurs is alcohol and sugar or other sweetening agents, as well as aromatic and coloring additives.

ALCOHOL The base spirit in liqueur production may be wine, grain, or fruit distillates, neutral liquors, or finished liquors.

SUGAR AND SWEETENING AGENTS Finely granulated refined sugar is what sweetens ninety-five percent of all liqueurs. Other sweetening agents are honey, glucose, and rock candy.

AROMATIC AGENTS The immense diversity of liqueurs can be attributed to a nearly boundless variety of natural aromatic substances. Countless plants, fruits, herbs, and barks, as well as their petals, peels, and seeds, find use as flavoring substances, and are processed in several different ways. Flavoring additives may be immersed in alcohol (maceration), or they may be distilled with the alcohol (infusion). Along with these two methods there are a number of other processes, some of which may be combined to introduce flavor to the liqueur. Finished products such as juice, tea, or coffee may also be used to impart flavor. Today many artificial essences are also used in liqueur production.

COLORING AGENTS One aspect that makes a liqueur appealing is its color. Among other substances that can serve as coloring agents are saffron, turmeric, and carrot, as well as various syrups and leaves, and of course non-hazardous artificial colors.

LIQUEUR AT THE BAR What makes many cocktails seem magically alluring is in no small degree their color, which may come from the liqueurs they are made with. Liqueurs are indispensable in mixing drinks, as a sweetener and to balance the flavor, and many classic cocktails, such as the Sidecar, White Lady, Margarita, Between the Sheets, or White Russian would be unimaginable without liqueurs.

Some classic mixing liqueurs are:

Cointreau, curaçao, Bénédictine, apricot brandy, Campari, Chartreuse, cherry brandy, crème de cacao (white and brown), crème de menthe (white and green), Drambuie, Grand Marnier, Galliano, Kahlúa, and maraschino.

Recent journals report that there is a renaissance of liqueurs. This is only true insofar as the increasing number of new fruit-flavored liqueurs and coloring agents offer new possibilities to create cocktails.

THE MOST IMPORTANT LIQUEUR GROUPS

The history of liqueur production goes back hundreds of years, and there is not only a multitude of different types and brands but also the most varied methods of production. Consequently, a definitive classification of the diverse liqueur types is next to impossible. The most important groups, however, are:

1. **Herb, spice, and bitter liqueurs**
2. **Fruit liqueurs**
3. **Crèmes**
4. **Emulsion liqueurs**
5. **Whisk(e)y liqueurs**

1. HERB, SPICE, AND BITTER LIQUEURS

Giving exact divisions within this category of liqueurs would be misleading. All have a long tradition and history behind them. Some of them are world-famous and have made their inventors wealthy. Shrouded in secrecy, their recipes have been passed down through time, and even today they are well guarded and known only to a few—often only to members of the family.

Originally many of these liqueurs were made in monasteries and sold as medicines, and today they are often still considered to have healing properties, with their hundreds of different herbs. Many countries are famous for their liqueurs, but Italy and France are the leaders not only in liqueur production but in consumption as well.

Cloister and herbal liqueurs are customarily served neat or on the rocks. They often make an ideal digestif and still serve the same original purpose: as a healing agent and medicine.

The best-known brands:

Amaretto di Saronno Originale–the most famous of all amaretto liqueurs; its distinct almond flavor comes from apricot stones, Italy, 56° proof

Averna Amaro Siciliano–amaro/herbal liqueur, Italy, 68° proof

Bénédictine D.O.M.–herbal-spice liqueur (world-famous liqueur from Fécamp, Normandy), France, 80° proof

Branca Menta–bitter liqueur/bitters with peppermint flavor, Italy, 80° proof

Calisay–herbal-bitter liqueur (cinchona), Spain, 66° proof

Centerbe (Mentuccia)–herbal liqueur with peppermint flavor, Italy, 60°–84° proof

Certosa–herbal liqueur, Italy

Chartreuse—cloister liqueur from Grenoble (130 herbs and a wine base), France; Jaune (yellow), 80° proof; Verte (green), 110° proof

China Martini—herbal liqueur (cinchona), Italy, 62° proof

Cordial Campari—Campari liqueur with raspberry flavor, Italy, 60° proof

Cuarenta y Tres (Licor 43)—herbal liqueur, Spain, 68° proof

Danziger Goldwasser—herbal liqueur (grain) with goldleaf, Poland, 76° proof

Escorial Grün—herbal liqueur, Germany, 112° proof

Fernet Branca—bitter liqueur/bitters, Italy, 84° proof

Galliano—herbal-spice liqueur with vanilla flavor, Italy, 70° proof

Izarra—herbal liqueur, France/Spain; yellow, 80° proof; green, 96° proof

Jägermeister—herbal liqueur, Germany, 70° proof

Mille Fiori—herbal liqueur, Italy, 90° proof

Ramazotti (Amaro)—herbal liqueur, Italy, 60° proof

Strega (Liquore Strega)—herbal liqueur, Italy, 80° proof

Suze—herbal liqueur (gentian), France, 80° proof

Underberg—bitter liqueur/bitters, Germany, 88° proof

Unicum—bitter liqueur/bitters, Hungary/Italy, 84° proof

BITTER APERITIFS The bitter aperitif Campari is, pure and simple, synonymous with the word aperitif. Its place of birth: Milan; year of birth: 1861; father: Caspare Davide Campari.

Equally famous are two classic cocktails based on Campari: the **Americano** and the **Negroni**.

Another classic aperitif is Aperol, produced since 1919 in Padua according to the same recipe. Its weak alcoholic strength at 22° proof, harmonious taste, and brilliant red color all contribute to its popularity.

Both of these bitter aperitifs are served on the rocks or mixed with soda. Their flavorful components make them very well suited for mixing, and they are exceptionally harmonious with juices and Mediterranean sweet wines.

Aperol—bitters of herbs, Italy, 22° proof

Campari—bitters of herbs and citrus fruits, Italy, 50° proof

Some other brands:
Cynar—bitters of herbs and artichoke, Italy/Switzerland, 33° proof

Suze à la Gentiane—gentian flavor, France, 40° proof

2. FRUIT LIQUEURS

Fruit juice liqueurs are liqueurs in which the flavor is determined by a fruit juice.

The taste of fruit-flavored liqueurs comes from fruits and parts of fruits such as their peels. (Triple sec, for example, is a fruit-flavored liqueur made from citrus fruits.)

Famous types:

Apricot brandy–brandy wine with apricot flavor, 60° proof

Blackberry brandy–blackberry liqueur, 50°–60° proof

Cherry brandy–brandy wine with cherry flavor, 60° proof (Cherry Heering from Denmark is the best-known brand, aged in wood casks)

Cointreau–triple sec, France, 80° proof (the number-one mixing liqueur at the bar)

Curaçao–general term for orange-flavored liqueurs (made from dried sour orange peels), Curaçao, West Indies, 70°–80° proof

Well known are:

Curaçao Triple Sec; Red Orange; Blue

Forbidden Fruit—fruit-flavored liqueur, 100° proof or greater (of various citrus fruits, such as grapefruit)

Grand Marnier—orange liqueur (Cognac), France, 80° proof

Kroatzbeere—blackberry liqueur, 50°–60° proof

Luxardo—cherry liqueur, Italy, 60°–70° proof

Maraschino—sour cherry liqueur, Dalmatia, 60°–70° proof

Peachtree (Original)—peach liqueur, Holland, 48° proof

3. Crèmes

These are very sweet liqueurs with a 28 percent sugar content. They are thick and excellent for mixing.

Crème de bananes—banana liqueur, white and brown, 50° proof

Crème de cacao—cocoa and vanilla liqueur, white and brown, 50° proof

Crème de café—coffee liqueur, 50° proof

Crème de cassis—black currant liqueur, most from Dijon, France, 50° proof

Crème de fraises—strawberry-herb liqueur, 50° proof

Crème de framboises—raspberry liqueur, 50° proof

Crème de mandarines—mandarine liqueur, 50° proof

Crème de menthe—peppermint liqueur, white and green, 60° proof

Crème de noisette—hazelnut liqueur, 56° proof

Crème de violette—violet liqueur, 50° proof (in English called crème Yvette)

4. EMULSION LIQUEURS

These are liqueurs in which chocolate (cocoa powder), cream, milk, and eggs, for example, are homogenized together with alcohol and sugar.

Famous types:

Advocaat—egg liqueur, Holland, 40° proof

Batida de coco—coconut milk liqueur, originally from Brazil, 40° proof

Batida de café—coffee liqueur, 40° proof

Batida de menthe—peppermint liqueur, 40° proof

Kahlúa—coffee liqueur (with herbs and vanilla), Mexico, produced in England for some European countries, 53° proof

Tia Maria—coffee liqueur (with sugar cane alcohol), originally from Jamaica, 53° proof

5. WHISK(E)Y LIQUEURS

Bailey's Irish Cream—chocolate flavored, Ireland, 34° proof

Drambuie—honey flavored, Scotland, 80° proof

Irish Mist—herb and honey flavored, Ireland, 70° proof

Southern Comfort—orange and peach flavored, United States, 80° proof

ANISÉES

Brandy wines and liqueurs flavored with aniseed are called
pastis in France and are usually served diluted with water.

Absinthe, the predecessor of anis, has been banned since
the 1920s because of the toxicity of the wormwood from which
it was made.

A few well-known anisées:

Anisette–herbal aniseed-flavored liqueur, France, 50° proof
(the brand Marie Brizard is famous)

Ouzo–aniseed-flavored brandy wine, Greece, 80°–100°
proof

Pastis–aniseed-flavored brandy wine, France,
80°–90° proof (Pernod, Ricard)

Raki–aniseed-flavored brandy wine
(marc, rose, and fig), Turkey, 80°–100°
proof

In Spain various anis liqueurs are also
known as **anisados**.

Sparkling Wines

Champagne

History In the seventeenth century in France (and England) lightly sparkling wines became the drink of fashion. They originated in France in the Champagne region and owed their unique quality to a second fermentation—originally unintentional—in the bottle. The long road leading this simple sparkling wine to the prized Champagne of today was certainly ridden with obstacles.

The **Benedictine monk Dom Pérignon** (1638–1715) made handsome profits from Champagne. The cellar master for the Abbaye Hautvilliers, he was an exceptional wine connoisseur for his time. He not only was the first vintner to press white wine from red grapes but also achieved great success in experiments blending different wines to create the so-called *cuvée* that is so important in Champagne production. He also had the idea of manipulating bottle fermentation by adding sweeteners and of retaining the resulting carbon dioxide in the bottle by using natural cork stoppers.

Dom Pérignon's methods were refined until the end of the nineteenth century and led to the modern method of producing Champagne. Today one of the great Champagnes bears the name Dom Pérignon.

PRODUCTION Only products that are cultivated in a strict legally defined area of France, pressed from certain grapes, and produced by the so-called *méthode champenoise* may be called Champagne.

CULTIVATION AREA The wine-growing region of about 82,000 acres (about 90 miles northeast of Paris) is distinguished by its unique chalk soil, which ensures a particular drainage and heat storage.

This area, of which 70,000 acres were being cultivated as of 1991, is subdivided into three principal districts:

> Montagne de Reims
> Vallée de la Marne (Epernay)
> Côtes des Blancs (Avize)

Less important than the actual area of origin is its particular position. Depending on the condition of the soil and the quality of the grapes harvested there, the vineyards of these districts are classified as grand cru, premier cru, and so forth. The higher the rating, the higher the price of the grapes. Premium Champagnes naturally contain a higher percentage of grand-cru wines than standard Champagnes.

GRAPE VARIETIES Champagne may be made from only the following varieties of grape:

Pinot Noir (black)
Pinot Meunier (black)
Chardonnay (white)

Traditionally Pinot Noir and Chardonnay are considered the better wines, but Pinot Meunier is steadily gaining influence, partly because this type of grape is more resilient and more profitable. To maintain standards of quality, the size of the harvest is set anew each year (about 4 to 6 tons per acre) and vine-trimming methods are legally defined as well.

Because the juice inside black grapes is also white, all three grape varieties may be blended. A distinction is made between Blanc de Noirs (Pinot Noir, Pinot Meunier) and the ever-popular Blanc de Blancs (Chardonnay).

Rosé Champagnes are often made by adding red wine, but they may also be made by allowing the must pressed from black grapes to remain on the grape skins longer, which allows it to absorb color.

MÉTHODE CHAMPENOISE Champagne is different from many other sparkling wines largely because it is required to undergo a second fermentation in the same bottle in which it will be sold. This process—*la méthode champenoise*—is as follows.

First a dry white **base wine** (*vin de cuvée*) is produced: the different grape varieties, separated by source, are pressed (a maximum of 150 liters of wine may be pressed from each ton of grapes) and fermented. Then follows an aging period of several months or sometimes several years in stainless-steel tanks (or traditionally in wooden casks).

The next step is crucial in determining the quality of the Champagne: **the blending of the cuvée** (*assemblage*). Up to fifty base wines from various locations and years are blended together to achieve the desired character of a particular Champagne. The blending of the cuvée is crucial to the success of a brand, and thus it is the pride and secret of each Champagne house.

After the assemblage comes **bottle fermentation**–the transformation of the cuvée into sparkling wine. After the addition of the *liqueur de tirage* (yeast and sugar dissolved in older wine), the cuvée is bottled in pressure-safe bottles, corked, and stored to age. The yeast causes the added sugar to convert into alcohol and carbon dioxide. This process results in residual substances (yeast deposits) that must later be removed. To achieve this the bottles are placed in **riddling stands** in which they are continually turned to loosen the sediments. Simultaneously the bottles are gradually raised to a vertical position until finally they are positioned upside-down (*sur pointes*) and the yeast deposits have settled into the bottle neck as a plug. The longer the Champagne matures with the yeast deposit, the richer its bouquet and the finer and more long-lasting its bubbles. (At least one year is required; for vintage Champagne three years; most, however, are aged considerably longer.)

Now the Champagne can be **degorged**, which requires immersing the neck of the bottle in a chilling solution until the yeast plug is frozen. The bottle is opened and the sediment shoots out. The inevitable loss of a certain amount of Champagne in

this process is compensated for with an addition of wine—as a rule from the same cuvée—and sugar (*dosage d'expédition*). The sugar content ultimately determines the taste of the finished Champagne.

European Community laws of 1974 and of 1985 differentiate the following levels of sweetening of Champagne:

TYPE	SUGAR CONTENT (*percent per liter*)	TASTE
Extra Brut	0–1.5% residual sugar	especially dry
Brut	1.5% residual sugar	very dry to dry
Extra Dry	1.2–2% residual sugar	dry to half-dry
Sec	2–3% residual sugar	half-dry to half-sweet
Demi-Sec	3–5% residual sugar	sweet
Doux	5%+ residual sugar	very sweet

After the addition of the *dosage d'expédition*, the newly corked Champagne is ready to be shipped. Because the yeast sediments have been removed, its basic character is not altered by long storage, although the bouquet can be nicely rounded off when a young Champagne is allowed to rest for one or two more years after the degorging.

VINTAGE CHAMPAGNE In years when the harvest is of particularly good quality, Champagne houses usually bottle vintage Champagne (in French, *millésimé*).

These too are composed of various base wines; however, the composition consists of wines only from the single year in question. Generally they are matured with the yeast much longer than the legal minimum requirement of three years.

The only Champagnes of comparable value are individual special or prestige cuvées, for which the Champagne houses likewise use strictly premium wines. These may be vintage wines or a blend of vintages.

BOTTLE SIZES

Quart (¹/₄ bottle) .2 liters

Demi (¹/₂ bottle) .375 liters

Bouteille (1 bottle) .75 liters

Magnum 1.5 liters

Jeroboam 3 liters

Rehoboam 4.5 liters

Methusalem 6 liters

Salmanazar 9 liters

Balthazar 12 liters

Nebuchadnezzar 15 liters

HANDLING CHAMPAGNE

Champagne should be stored in a horizontal position at a temperature between 50°F and 55°F and served at a temperature between 43 and 47°F, which is best achieved by placing the bottle into a wine bucket with ice and water. Champagne is often poorly handled: it loves dark, cool cellars and a consistent temperature; it loves clean Champagne flutes (not cocktail glasses that allow its bouquet to evaporate) that are completely free of dishwashing liquid. It deplores artificial light and rapid chilling in the freezer, frosted glasses, and the swizzle stick, which in a matter of minutes will destroy what nature and the skilled cellar master have spent years to create.

CHAMPAGNE BRANDS—A selection of important houses and the wares they sell:

Bollinger (founded 1829)—family enterprise, produces mainly from its own vineyards; sold as Special Cuvée Brut; Grande Année Brut; RD Extra Brut; Année Rare RD

Deutz & Geldermann (1838)—family enterprise, Blanc de Blancs (vintage and nonvintage); La Cuvée W. Deutz

Krug (1843)—for these Champagnes the first fermentation still takes place in wooden fermenting vats; Grand Cuvée; Rosé; Vintage; Clos du Mesnil (vintage Blanc de Blancs)

Laurent-Perrier (1812)—family enterprise; Brut; Rosé Brut; Ultra Brut; Cuvée Grand Siècle; Millésime Rare

Moët et Chandon (1743)–the world market leader; Brut Imperial; Brut Imperial Vintage; Brut Imperial Rosé. From this house too comes the cuvée **Dom Pérignon**–produced only in good years–which is also offered as a rosé.

Joseph Perrier (1825)–Brut (vintage and nonvintage); Cuvée du Cent Cinquantenaire

Perrier-Jouet (1811)–Extra Dry; Grand Brut; Brut Vintage; Brut Vintage Rosé

Piper-Heidsieck (1885)–Brut Extra; Brut Millésime Rare (vintage); Brut Sauvage (without sweetener, vintage)

Pommery & Greno (1836)—about 50 percent from its own vineyards, exclusively Grand Cru; Pommery Brut Royal; Pommery Brut Rosé; Pommery Brut Vintage; Louise Pommery Vintage White; Louise Pommery Vintage Rosé

Roederer (1860)—family enterprise, produces mainly from its own vineyards; Brut Premier; Brut Rosé; Brut Cristal (vintage)

Ruinart (1729)—the oldest Champagne house, belongs now to Moët & Chandon; Brut; Millésime; Blanc de Blancs; and Rosé (vintage)

Taittinger (1734)—family enterprise; Brut; Brut Réserve; Taittinger Collection; Comtes de Champagne Blanc de Blancs and Rosé (vintage)

Veuve Clicquot Ponsardin (1771)—Brut; La Grande Dame; Carte d'Or (vintage)

Other brands: **Ayala, Billecart-Salmon, Alfred Gratien, Charles Heidsieck, Heidsieck & Co., Monopole, Lanson, Mercier, Napoléon, B. Paillard, Pol Roger, Salon**

FRENCH CRÉMANT

French *méthode champenoise* sparkling wines that are made out-side of Champagne are called Crémant (as of 1994). These wines also come from specific cultivation areas (*Appellation Controlée*).

Crémant d'Alsace
Crémant de Bordeaux
Crémant de Bourgogne
Crémant de Die
Crémant de Limoux
Crémant de Loire

The minimum maturing period with the yeast present is nine months, but grape varieties differ from region to region.

GERMAN SEKT

With a consumption per person of six bottles annually, the Germans are the world champions of sparkling wine con-sumers. The most popular type sold is German sekt, followed by the Italian spumante and French sparkling wines, including Champagne (whose consumption has nearly tripled in the last ten years—to 13 million bottles sold in 1989).

Sparkling wine production in Germany is nearly as old as in France: toward the end of the eighteenth century German cellar masters and tradespeople, who had learned their business in France, began to produce it in Germany. The first sekt manufacturer was the cellar master **Kessler**, a student of the widow Clicquot, who founded his own firm in 1826 in Esslingen.

Renowned sekt cellars founded in the mid-nineteenth century are still in operation today: **Henkell** (1832), **Mathäus Müller** (1838), **Deinhard** (1843), **Kupferberg** (1850), **Söhnlein** (1864).

The term *sekt* became popular in its time through a joke: in 1825 the actor Ludwig Devrient, still in full costume and still immersed in the role of Falstaff after a stage performance,

stepped into his local tavern and demanded, "Bring me sekt, scoundrel!" But the waiter did not bring him sherry sack (which had been translated in the German edition of Shakespeare as "sekt"), but the drink Devrient always consumed: Champagne.

TANK FERMENTATION Until well into the twentieth century sekt was produced by the *méthode champenoise*. It was not until the 1950s that the more economical tank fermentation method emerged, making the mass production of today possible.

In this process the second fermentation too takes place in a tank of enormous capacity, which allows the costly riddling and degorging procedures to be dispensed with. After one month the wine and yeast can be separated and filtered under pressure. Ninety-five percent of German sekt is produced by this method. Some quality-conscious manufacturers dedicated to maintaining tradition do, however, still produce it by the costly Champagne method.

TRANSFER PROCESS In this procedure the second fermentation still takes place in the bottle; the wine is not degorged, however, but filtered under pressure through a filtering system and then rebottled into new bottles. Products made by this method may also be sold with the description "bottle fermented."

VINTNERS' SEKT These are sekts made by vintners, either independently or as part of a vintners' association, exclusively by the *méthode champenoise*. Only indigenous and often vintner-owned wines are processed in these sekts.

GRAPE VARIETIES The best types of grape for sekt are Riesling and Chardonnay. However, only 20 percent of the grapes that are processed for sekt are grown in Germany; the large remainder is supplied in the form of wines from France, Italy, and various other countries. Sekt manufacturers purchase in part virtually the cheapest wines; in part, however, they also purchase wines of good quality. The price of a bottle of sekt can be taken as a halfway reliable measure of the quality of the base wines it is made of.

ITALIAN SPUMANTE

The oldest Italian sparkling wine is **Asti Spumante** (first sold in 1865 by Carlo Gancia). It is pressed from aromatic Muscat grapes and manufactured by the *metodo rurale,* which means it is fermented only once, and thus contains less carbon dioxide and more grape sugar, making it sweet. The alcoholic strength is low—a mere 9 percent. The majority of spumante wines are produced by the vat process (tank fermentation), although in Italy there is also a growing number of houses that make it exclusively by the *metodo classico* (*méthode champenoise*). They are united under the Istituto Spumante Classico in Milan and process only select grapes from delimited regions.

CULTIVATION AREAS Franciacorta (Brescia), Trentino/Alto Adige, Oltrepo Pavese

GRAPE VARIETIES Mostly Chardonnay and Pinot Bianco; to a smaller extent Pinot Nero and Pinot Grigio are also used.

The maturation period with the yeast must be at least fifteen months (for vintage spumante, two years), and the alcoholic strength is 12 percent.

Spumantes contain up to 9 percent sugar by volume, and even the dry types of spumante have a relatively high sugar content—up to 3 percent.

PROSECCO is a variety of grape from Veneto that to a small extent is also double fermented and processed into spumante. Only rarely does this wine achieve the quality of the customary spumante.

Spumante brands:
Ca' del Bosco
Cesarini Sforza
Ferrari
Livio Felluga
Prosecco Rustica

SPANISH CAVA

Sparkling wine has been produced since 1872 in Spain, or to be more precise, in Catalonia. This wine, called *cava*, is produced exclusively by the *méthode champenoise* and is matured with the yeast for between nine months and four years.

AREAS OF CULTIVATION Penedès (15 miles southwest of Barcelona, distributes 90 percent of the grapes used), Conca de Barberà, Raimat

GRAPE VARIETIES Parellada, Macabeo, Xarello, Chardonnay (white).

PRODUCTION The largest and oldest cava house is the firm of **Codorniu** (founded in 1872 by José Raventós in Sant Sadurni d'Anoia), followed by **Freixenet**. Both houses own the largest bottle-fermenting cellars in the world, and each sells about 60 million bottles annually (a point of comparison: Moët & Chandon sells 25 million annually).

Other brands:
Juvé y Camps Castellblanch
Marques de Monistrol

U.S. SPARKLING WINES

Sparkling wine has been made in the United States for more than a century. European winemaking techniques, including the *méthode champenoise,* were freely borrowed by pioneering winemakers, along with European place names. As a result, the term *Champagne* can be used on a U.S. sparkling wine (even bulk-process wines) so long as it is preceded by an indication of origin (California, etc.). Although bulk-process bubbly dominates the market, high-quality U.S. sparkling wines have been made since the 1960s from classic Champagne varieties

(Pinot Noir and Chardonnay), notably in Northern California.

In fact, a number of French Champagne producers, including **Moët-Hennessy**, **Piper-Heidsieck**, **Taittinger**, **Deutz**, and **Mumm**, now produce excellent sparkling wine in California. Understandably, none of them use the term *Champagne* on their labels.

Principal *méthode champenoise* producers:

Domaine Carneros
Domaine Chandon
Iron Horse
Jordan
Maison Deutz
Mumm Napa Valley
Piper-Sonoma
Scharffenberger
Schramsberg

OTHER SPARKLING WINES

The United States is not the only country outside Europe that produces high-quality sparkling wines. Australia, South Africa, and New Zealand all make excellent but limited quantities of *méthode champenoise* wines.

FORTIFIED WINES

VERMOUTH

Vermouth is the name that is given to wine **infused** with herbs, alcohol, sugar, caramel, and water according to specific proprietary recipes in Italy and France.

WINE A minimum of 70 percent of vermouth consists of a meticulous blend of various white wines, usually dry.

ALCOHOL The base-wine mixture is brought to the prescribed strength (15 to 18 percent) by the addition of pure grape brandy. The alcohol also functions as a preservative.

HERBS The flavor and character of vermouth depend mainly on the herbal extract it contains. This is what gives vermouth its appetite-arousing and digestive effect. A multitude of aromatic herbs and spices—most importantly wormwood338—are added to the alcohol and extracted (maceration). The exact mix of herbs (most known as healing agents) remains the guarded secret of each producer.

SUGAR rounds off the flavor; it subdues the bitterness of many herbs and also acts as a bonding agent for the flavors. Caramel gives vermouth its yellowish to red color.

WATER All ingredients are mixed together with water, which, however, may not make up more than 15 percent of the vermouth by volume.

TYPES OF VERMOUTH A distinction is made between sweet and dry vermouth:

Sweet vermouth is white (bianco) or red (rosso) and is 15–16 percent alcohol by volume; it contains up to 15 percent residual sugar.

Dry vermouth is white (dry, extra dry), usually 18 percent alcohol, and contains at most 5 percent residual sugar.

Half-sweet vermouth is sold as a rosé.

HISTORY Vermouth has a long history. It presumably began shortly after the invention of wine. Like many spirits, vermouth was originally used as a medicine, because it was discovered very early that a healing agent could be created by adding herbs to alcohol. The Italians were the first to capitalize on this and made vermouth popular. Turin and its surrounding area became the center of vermouth production, and today the largest producers are still situated here, such as the firm Carpano, which sold vermouth as early as the end of the eighteenth century.

VERMOUTH AT THE BAR Long valued for its healing properties, vermouth grew to be—first in Italy's aperitif bars—the star of the aperitif hour. It is served neat, on the rocks, in a mix of different vermouths, with a lemon twist or orange peel, or mixed with the other popular spirits from its native country, such as Campari.

Vermouth ultimately became world-famous as a component of the **dry Martini**; once the equal partner of gin, today it has been forsaken because of popular trends or ignorance on the part of bar guests and the disrespect of many bartenders—humbled, it is often only poured over ice and then dumped out. Let's stick together at last and give vermouth its pride and purpose back: **without dry vermouth—no dry Martini! Without dry vermouth—naked gin!**

(For the bartender: when a customer orders a Martini always ask whether he or she means a Martini cocktail or a vermouth made by the firm Martini.)

Vermouth brands:

Three vermouth houses lead the world market: **Martini & Rossi**, **Cinzano** (both Turin), and **Noilly Fils & Co.** (France). From the latter comes the driest of all vermouths, **Noilly Prat**. (The dryness is fairly perceptible in this vermouth, and it is the only one that should be used to make a dry Martini.) Other brands are **Punt è Mes** from the firm of Carpano and the French **Picon**.

SHERRY

Sherry is a fortified wine from a precisely designated cultivation area that is restricted to the towns of Jerez de la Frontera, Sanlúcar de Barrameda, and Puerto de Santa Maria in the Cádiz province (Andalusia) of Spain. The largest part (70 percent) of the area is known as **Jerez Superior** and is distinguished by its mild climate and white chalk soil (*albarizas*), which retains water well, ensuring ample moistness even in the summer months. The remaining area consists of clay soil called *barros* and to a smaller extent of sandy soil (*arenas*), which are only suitable for growing Moscatel grapes.

GRAPE VARIETIES · Sherry is produced exclusively from white grapes. The largest percentage (95 percent) are the **Palomino** grapes, but **Pedro Ziménes** and **Moscatel**, which are used only in blending sweet sherries, also come into play.

PRODUCTION To increase the sugar content of the must, and therefore the alcohol content in the wine, the grapes may be placed for a period in the blazing sunlight so that some of their juice will evaporate.

Fermentation used to take place in oak casks. Today most sherries are fermented in stainless steel, cement, or fiberglass tanks, which may be cooled. By maintaining a consistent temperature between 72°F and 79°F, the conversion of the sugar, which takes longer than when fermented in a wooden cask, is more effective, and the process of sunning the grapes is not always necessary.

After fermentation, sherry barrels are filled to just 80 percent of their capacity so that the wine has enough room to develop a yeast scum known as *flor*. This scum builds on the surface of the wine as a result of the specific properties of the Palomino grape. This process is crucial to the development of certain sherry flavors.

After development of flor, the wines are categorized: the lighter, pale wines are called *finos;* strong, heavy sherry known as *oloroso* is produced when there is little or no flor development. These are the two basic types.

FINO These wines are fortified with grape brandy to about 15½ percent alcohol, and they are matured for one to two years under the flor. This phase is called **añada**. The wine is blended and aged by the **solera method**, in which the añada wines of different vintages are mixed in order to maintain a consistent quality and taste over years. The casks are arranged in three to four long rows by year so that the oldest wine is at the bottom and the youngest at the top. Wine is taken only from the bottommost row, without ever completely emptying the casks. The wine that is taken out is replaced with wine from the row above, and that with wine from the row above it, and so on. The topmost row is filled from the añada casks. The average age of a normal fino is generally about five years, and of course contains a portion of very many older wines.

The finished fino has an alcoholic strength of 15 percent to 18 percent alcohol and is the dryest of all sherries, with a light golden color, and a delicate almond aroma. It is considered a **classic aperitif**.

MANZANILLA is a fino from Sanlúcar de Barremeda; at 15–16 percent alcohol it is the lightest of sherries, fresh and aromatic, and with an attractive bitter bite.

AMONTILLADO is an aged fino that derives its special hazelnut flavor from undergoing a second maturation process without flor after the customary maturation by the solera method. The flor dies off if the fino is matured without having any further wines added to it or if its alcoholic strength is raised again to 18 percent. A great difference in quality may arise depending on how old the base finos are (up to five years) and how long they mature without flor (more than seven years). Inexpensive amontillados are usually blends of less valuable finos and olorosos that have not undergone a second maturation.

Amontillado is amber colored, mild flavored, and actually dry, although for exports it is usually somewhat sweetened. It is offered as both **medium** and **medium dry**.

OLOROSO The alcohol content of these sherrys is also increased after the fermentation, up to 18 percent, which kills off the flor. They remain for up to ten years in the añada, which allows the alcoholic strength to rise up to 24 percent.

Olorosos, too, are matured by the solera method and are once more categorized: the strongest are degraded as **raya** and processed into cream sherry; **palo cortado**, a rarity, is particularly aromatic, and has a taste somewhere between oloroso and amontillado. The large amount of remaining wine is made into actual oloroso, which is dark brown, heavy-bodied, and has a rich walnut flavor.

CREAM Cream sherrys are olorosos (raya) blended with sweet wine. The best sweet wine comes from the **Pedro Ximénez** grape. It is made by adding brandy shortly after the fermentation begins, halting the conversion of sugar into alcohol; the resulting dark, syrupy wine then spends a year aging by the solera method. It is relatively expensive and sometimes is bottled by itself.

Another kind of sweet wine is **mistela**. It is produced the same way as Pedro Ximénez, although from **Palomino** grapes, which are more abundant and thus more economical.

The simplest sweet wine is made from the **Moscatel** grape; this wine has an intense, flowery aroma and is not made by the solera method.

The quality of a cream sherry may vary, depending on whether it is made from a young oloroso that was blended with simple sweet wine or an aged oloroso containing up to 10 percent Pedro Ximénez.

Sugar content:
A differentiation is made between
Dry (less than 1 percent),
Medium dry (1–5 percent)
Medium sweet (5–10 percent), and
Cream (10–14 percent)

SHERRY AT THE BAR There are only a few sherry connoisseurs outside Spain, and unfortunately very few of them seem to be knowledgeable—all they know is that there is dry sherry and sweet sherry!

Sherrys should be stored in a cool, dark place, but not for too long a time. Finos and manzanillas are especially sensitive and lose their character after even just a year from when they are bottled. Opened bottles of finos and manzanillas should not be kept for longer than a week, and olorosos and creams should not be kept longer than a month after they have been opened. Premium sherrys are served neat, preferably in small copitas, the classic sherry glass. The serving temperature for finos and manzanillas is generally between 47° and 53°F; for amontillados, olorosos, and creams, 65°F. **To make a mixed drink from sherry, combine different sherrys and mix them with vermouth.**

Large sherry producers:
Gonzáles Byass—Fino Tio Pepe
John Harvey & Sons—Bristol Cream; "1796" Palo Cortado
Pedro Domecq—Fino La Ina; Rio Viejo Dry Oloroso
Sandeman—Don Fino
    The largest sherry houses are also the largest producers of Spanish brandy.

MADEIRA

Madeira is a fortified wine that is made only on the Portuguese island of the same name in the Atlantic. Distinguishing features of the island of Madeira are its volcanic soil and a stable climate (never below 60°F or above 77°F).

PREDOMINANT WINE VARIETIES

Malmsey—sweetest and best Madeira
Boal, Bual—a light, somewhat less sweet wine
Verdelho—half-dry, light honey flavor
Sercial—the driest Madeira

The **addition of alcohol** occurs either during fermentation (the conversion of the sugar is thus stopped, leaving the wine sweet) or after (the sugar is completely converted into alcohol, making the wine dry).

Madeira's unique character comes from being **baked**, so to speak: the wine is heated in special ovens (estufas) for a minimum of three months at 122°F, which causes it to take on a honey-sweet caramel aroma. Premium sweet products are heated for a longer period at 104°F. After it is baked, the wine matures for about three years. After it undergoes the **solera method** (see Sherry), it is blended and again fortified with brandy until it reaches an alcoholic strength of 18–22 percent. Now the actual maturing period of the madeira begins, and it must remain in the cask for at least eight years. Madeira can— even in the bottle—improve significantly with age.

A famous brand:
Leacock (owned by the British Madeira Wine Company Ltd., the largest Madeira producer and exporter)

PORT

The history of port begins in the second half of the seventeenth century. From the very beginning the port wine business was securely in the hands of the British. Many famous port wine houses of today still bear British names.

The home of the wines that go into port lies in northern Portugal, along the upper Douro River and its neighboring valleys. This fifty-mile stretch was clearly delineated some two hundred years ago, and the current borders were legally defined in 1907.

The Douro Valley comprises approximately 600,000 acres. About a tenth of that is used for vineyards. There are 25,000 vintners residing in this area, and there are some 85,000 vineyards.

The vineyards in the Douro are noteworthy for their many grape varieties.

PRINCIPAL GRAPE VARIETIES Touriga Francesa, Tinta Roriz, Tinto Cáo, Touriga Nacional, Tinta Barroca

CLIMATE AND SOIL The climatic and geological conditions for making outstanding wines complement each other here like no other place in the world.

The Douro Valley is protected from the Atlantic winds by its high mountain range. Brutally hot summers and very cold, often very rainy winters result in a particular ripeness in the grapes.

The ground in the vineyards provides another condition for growing exceptional wines. It consists primarily of shale that does not lie horizontally, as it usually does, but at an angle of 60–90 degrees toward the center of the earth. This prevents the rays of the sun from penetrating very deeply into the soil day after day. The shale stores the warmth, which it can emit even until late in the night.

The harvest begins in mid-September and can last into October.

FERMENTATION Centrifuges and fermentation tanks have largely replaced the open cement *lagares* in which the grapes used to be pressed by foot. Today the grapes are immediately heaped into a machine that mashes them and removes the stems. The mass of mashed grapes is then pumped into a large cement container, which is filled within two days and then sealed. During this time the must is kept cool to prevent premature fermentation.

After a short time enough heat is generated in the

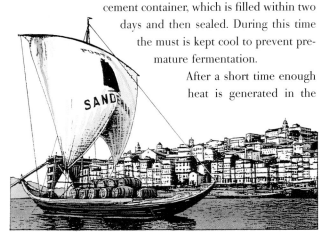

container to start the fermentation. If half of the sugar in the must converts, that is, when the mash has an alcohol content  of about 8 percent by volume, it is pressed and the must is pumped into containers where it then ferments.

Depending on how sweet the resulting wine should be, the cellar master stops the fermentation by adding a 150° proof grape brandy in a ratio of about 1 part brandy to 5 parts grape must. This increases the alcohol content to about 20 percent by volume and leaves about 9–10 percent residual grape sugar.

Port production necessitates a longer cask maturation, because a harmonious flavor in the blend of wine and brandy can only be achieved gradually. To accomplish this, the port wines are brought to **Vila Nova de Gaia**.

Today growers sell their grapes to port wine firms who prepare the wine in their own wine-pressing houses in the Douro region. Occasionally a vintner might prepare the wine in his own location.

THE ENTREPOT (middle maturation period) Opposite the city of Porto, across the Douro River, lies Vila Nova de Gaia. This city is deeply involved in port wine because this is where the **Entrepot of Gaia** is located—the area where port wine houses have their cellars.

Shortly after harvesting, the wine, along with a certificate of its origin, is brought to this area. The Entrepot of Gaia is precisely defined and is supervised by the Instituto do Vinho do Porto, which is responsible for the control and quality of port wine. In the Entrepot of Gaia the wine ages until it has achieved the state of perfection that has made it world-famous. All port wine firms—currently there are fifty-eight—own ware-houses there, many of which are open to the public.

TYPES OF PORT

Most types of port are aged in the cask to develop their char-acter. These are called "wood ports," and they are ready to drink when bottled and shipped. Vintage port is the excep-tion—it is aged only two years in the cask and is intended to be aged further in the bottle to develop its character.

WHITE PORT White port wine matures for several years in wooden casks before it is bottled. Its popularity is still rather limited, but attempts to establish it as an aperitif have been moderately successful.

VINTAGE PORT Vintage port is the king of port wines and has brought fame and esteem to its homeland and its port wine houses.

Vintage port is made from wines from various locations and several wine-growing estates (*quintas*)—all from a **single exceptional year**.

Port wine producers decide individually if they wish to "declare" a vintage, whose quality must be approved by the port wine institute. On average, only three or four vintage years are declared per decade, although not all producers agree on the same years.

Great vintage years have occurred very seldom in this century. Only about 3 percent of the production of famous port wine houses such as Taylor, Graham, Warre, Fonseca, Nieport, Noval, and Cockburn end up as vintage port, and it is increasingly difficult to find these.

Vintage port must be decanted! Vintage ports are bottled after two years of cask maturing—they continue to age in the bottle, and precipitate a heavy deposit with time (vintage ports can age for twenty, thirty, even forty years in a cool cellar). To decant, first stand the bottle upright for a few hours in a dark, cool place. Remember that several days after it is opened vintage port loses its aroma.

It is a sin to mix vintage port with anything else.

The label of a vintage port wine must bear the harvest year and the description "Vintage."

Great years for vintage port: 1900, 1908, 1912, 1931, 1935, 1945, 1947, 1948, 1955, 1963, 1966, 1970, 1977, 1983, 1985, 1991, 1992.

1931 is reputed to be the port vintage of the century.

SINGLE QUINTA VINTAGE Also a true vintage port; the difference is that the wine comes from a **single wine-growing estate**. Typically, it is lighter than a port shipper's normal vintage, and is from good but not exceptional years.

LATE BOTTLED VINTAGE Wine from a vintage that is not bottled until the fourth to sixth year (i.e., it matures twice as long as vintage port), making it ready to drink when bottled.

The harvest year and the abbreviation LBV or the description "Late Bottled Vintage" must appear on the label of this wood port, which cannot be expected to have the character of a true vintage port.

COLHEITA Although this is a vintage wine from a single harvest, it does not achieve the quality of a good vintage port. It remains in the cask far longer than vintage port (at least seven years), and is therefore essentially a vintage tawny. It is ready to drink when bottled. It may, however, develop a deposit.

The label bears the harvest year and data about the bottling, as well as the declaration that it is cask-aged.

CRUSTED PORT (poor man's vintage) Although it is considered to have a vintage port character, this is a **port blend mixture of several vintages**. It is, however, bottled after two or three years and is ready to drink after three to four years, although the deposit (crust) must be removed. The label lists the date of the bottling.

WOOD PORT is a collective term for wines that are cask aged, which includes ruby, tawny, white, late bottled vintage, and crusted. They are the basis of all port wine houses' trade. They undergo their **full maturing period in the cask**, which means that once they are bottled, they hardly change at all.

Wood ports are a **blend** of wines from several years and different locations and never achieve the quality of vintage ports. Large houses do, however, market excellent wood ports (tawnys), which often have matured in the cask for twenty years or even longer.

RUBY Young, red, sweet port that often is matured in the cask for only three years. It is a blend of several vintages.

TAWNY Long cask aging, which results in a light to yellowish gold color, also gives tawny port a character that is not as sweet as a ruby port (oxidation alters the color and refines the flavor). Port wine houses place great value on producing exceptional tawny, and they are, in fact, often of excellent quality. Outstanding tawnys, which often age in the cask for twenty or more years, of course cannot be sold inexpensively. Although blends of various vintages, they can be labeled with age indications—"20 years old," etc. Vintage port fans should try an "old tawny" sometime.

HOW AND WHEN SHOULD PORT BE DRUNK? I am fundamentally opposed to mixing port wine with anything else. One exception, however, is white port, which is little known and which makes an excellent aperitif wine when chilled. If white port is to be mixed, it is most harmonious with other fortified wines such as vermouth and sherry.

I think it is wonderful when an old, fully matured tawny is served with cheese or as a digestif at the close of a fine meal.

Churchill was fond of relaxing with a bottle of port wine (presumably vintage) and a Havana cigar.

PORT WINE—MY SECRET LOVE In my long career as a bartender I have not poured so much as ten bottles of port wine at the bar.

And even so my heart belongs to port wine. Over the years I have collected a little secret treasure of ports that I have not broken into. If I'm ever down in the dumps, I pay my collection a visit, carefully pick up one of the bottles and raise it high to admire it under a diffuse light, and then gently return it to its place. Some will not be fully matured and ready to drink until the year 2000. And some, I hope, will remain unopened and achieve a biblical age.

Port wine connoisseurs and aficionados are rare, and even large restaurants usually have a modest selection. **The number-one port wine consumer is France.** However, only the mass-produced younger ports, mostly ruby ports, are sold and consumed in France.

The number-one port wine connoisseurs are its "inventors," the British. British merchants, producers, and auction houses have the port wine business firmly in their grasp (the most respected port wine houses are British owned).

Tawny is a British favorite. Most British people who keep a stock of liquor have at least a few bottles of vintage port in the cellar and bring them out of hiding on more than just special occasions. To the dismay of the British port wine fan club, the Americans and Japanese have begun to buy up the small supply of vintage products, causing their prices to gradually grow exorbitant.

THE ARTISTRY OF MIXING DRINKS AND COCKTAILS

"A GOOD COCKTAIL DOESN'T MEAN A BIG ONE."

Neither the amount of alcohol nor the amount of liquids in a cocktail is what is most important; balance is what counts.

Why doesn't every bartender mix good cocktails? Without experience and knowledge about the ingredients in a cocktail, it's impossible. Without conscientiousness, without a love of the profession, without discipline, it simply can't be done. **Ingenuity combined with a touch of inspiration makes the difference!**

PREREQUISITES FOR A PERFECT COCKTAIL

The best-quality ingredients! And that means brand-name liquors, fresh juices, etc. It's not a matter of quantity, but quality! Even professionals should occasionally remind themselves that cocktails as a rule should be made of no more than three ingredients and that only in the rarest cases is a cocktail improved by combining many ingredients.

Precise knowledge of the ingredients! What goes together? Which ingredients should be handled with care? There are so-called mixing guides that show exactly which ingredients are harmonious and which should not be shaken together. This may be helpful to some, but of what use would such a table be to a professional? Experienced bartenders read recipes and know whether a combination is possible without even having tasted it.

Understanding of the effect and "hour" of a cocktail! Bartenders and bars have often gone down in history for having created the ideal cocktail for certain occasions. Many classic drinks have been created in the simple daily routine of the bar at the right moment with the right guests at the right time.

Many cocktails can be categorized into groups of drinks according to which "hour" and opportunity they are best suited to. For example, there are aperitifs, digestifs, pick-me-up drinks, and corpse-reviver cocktails. Cocktails can stimulate the appetite as well as one's spirits or conclude a meal. They can refresh and enliven. They can also loosen the tongue of the taciturn, create friendships, or help us forget our troubles and make everything appear in a better light.

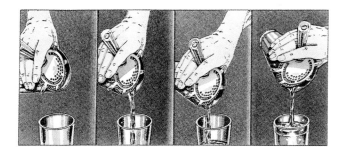

A good bartender should be aware of all this, and remember that if a cocktail is served in an appetizing and attractive manner, it must be prepared perfectly.

WHAT IS A COCKTAIL MADE OF?

The ingredients in a cocktail can be divided into three parts:
Basis, modifier, flavoring agent

1. THE BASIS Many cocktail recipe books arrange their recipes according to the liquor that forms the basis of the drink. This is nearly always the predominant ingredient.

This is usually also the **largest portion of the liquid** in the drink. It is the ingredient that determines the type of the cocktail. The basis and the largest ingredient in a Whiskey Sour, for example, is whiskey; in a Gimlet, gin; and in a Daiquiri, rum. Of course two harmonious liquors may also constitute the basis of a drink. In rare cases three liquors equally form the basis of a cocktail.

2. THE MODIFIER The modifying agent is the **second most important** part of a mixed drink. This must not, however, be so dominant as to alter the type of cocktail it goes in! The whiskey cocktail should remain a *whiskey* cocktail and the gin cocktail a *gin* cocktail.

The modifier is the ingredient that combines with the basis liquor, and together with it determines the direction of the flavor of the cocktail. Lacking this ingredient, a drink is not a cocktail, but only shaken or stirred liquor. Modifiers are primarily spirits blended with wines, juices, water, or sodas.

3. THE FLAVORING AGENT This third element in the cocktail is the **smallest in terms of amount**. Despite its small portion—often only a dash or two—it brings that certain something to the cocktail. It rounds it off and brings it to completion. This third ingredient often determines the color—from vibrant to delicate—and the flavor—from sweet to dry to bitter. **Special caution** is to be taken in using this ingredient; a little too much can ruin the cocktail.

The **flavoring and aromatic and coloring agent can be the smallest amount of liquors, liqueurs, syrups, or bitters.**

SHAKING

Many shakers are made of stainless steel or silver. I prefer the **Boston shaker**, which consists of a glass shaker that is somewhat smaller than its accompanying metal shaker. To ensure that the ingredients mix thoroughly, the glass part of the shaker should never be filled to the rim. **Never shake more than two cocktails at once in the Boston shaker.**

To prepare just one cocktail, five or six ice cubes should be placed in the shaker, and for two cocktails, three or four.

For some tropical drinks that I do not prepare in a blender, I use a shaker with crushed ice, which helps the ingredients to mix more thoroughly and makes the cocktail colder, but not as ice-cold and harsh on the stomach as frozen cocktails.

The glass part of the Boston shaker can also be used as a mixing glass.

THE ORDER OF MIXING THE INGREDIENTS There are differences of opinion about this. Personally, I begin least frequently with the alcohol and would advise the bartending novice to do the same. To make a Whiskey Sour, for example, I begin with lemon juice, add sugar to it, and add the whiskey last. Because lemon juice is not always of the same strength, I am cautious in sweetening it and cannot always use the exact same amount. Some guests who order a sour would in fact rather have a sweeter cocktail.

HOW LONG SHOULD A COCKTAIL BE SHAKEN? For drinks whose ingredients mix easily, **ten seconds** is sufficient.

Drinks with ingredients that are composed of elements that do not mix so readily (such as eggs or syrups) should be shaken for about twenty seconds.

STIRRING

Which cocktails should be prepared in a mixing glass?

1. All cocktails whose ingredients mix easily, but which must be served ice-cold (professional bars have a compartment in which cocktail glasses are chilled).

2. All cocktails that would become murky if shaken. Cocktails that are stirred are often among the classics (such as the Martini and the Manhattan).

About six ice cubes are placed in the mixing glass and stirred with a long barspoon (I use it upside down).

The stirring should be done from the bottom up. (The ice in the mixing glass is not put to further use!)

STIRRING COCKTAILS IN THE GLASS IN WHICH THEY ARE SERVED

First and foremost it is cocktails that mix well and that have nothing to gain by being shaken that are stirred in the glass in which they are served. These are mostly cocktails:

with a single liquor and a juice

(such as Gin Orange or Vodka Orange),

or

liquors that are mixed with soda

(such as Gin & Tonic or Vodka Lemon),

or

liquors that are mixed with Champagne or sparkling wine

(such as Champagne Orange or Champagne Campari),

or

cocktails in which two liquors are stirred together over ice, such as Scotch and Drambuie (Rusty Nail) or vodka and Kahlúa (Black Russian).

PREPARING COCKTAILS IN A BLENDER

Mixing cocktails with a blender is not universally popular. But since tropical drinks have come to enjoy increasing popularity, no bar can do without a blender. (I admit I'm not particularly fond of this method of preparation.)

For cocktails and drinks requiring fruits that must be pureed (such as fruit daiquiris) a blender is of course helpful and practically indispensable. But because they are ice-cold, all frozen drinks present a real trial for the stomach.

When mixing in a blender, I always use crushed ice. I place a bar scoop of crushed ice into the blender, then pour in the ingredients (or pieces of fruit), run the blender for about ten seconds at low speed, then switch to high speed and let it run for another ten seconds. (If a very thick cocktail is desired, add another half bar scoop of crushed ice before switching to high speed.)

For anyone who is inexperienced using a blender it can be a big help to first pour all the ingredients together into a glass.

For all drinks that are mixed in a blender the portion of sweet ingredients such as sugared water or syrup should be increased a bit.

BAR MEASUREMENTS

In this book cocktails and drink recipes are given in ounces.

The international standard size of a cocktail is up to 2 oz. Stirring or shaking on ice adds about another ¹/₂ oz.

Tall drinks contain 5 oz or more.

Medium cocktails are about 3 oz.

Liquors served neat or on the rocks are 1¹/₂ oz.

Wines vary from 3 to 5 oz.

The most important international bar measures:

1 dash
1 barspoon
¹/₄ fluid ounce = 0.7 cl
¹/₂ fl. oz = 1.4 cl
1 fl. oz (pony ounce) = 2.8 cl
1¹/₂ fl. oz = 4.2 cl
2 fl. oz = 5.6 cl

1 jigger (gill) = 1¹/₂ fl. oz
1 tablespoon = ¹/₂ fl. oz

BAR EQUIPMENT

Shaker

Mixing glass

Blender

Strainer—whether a drink is made in a shaker or in a mixing glass, it is strained into serving glasses. The sole purpose of this utensil is to keep the ice out of the drink. Because of its flexible spiral coil the strainer fits every size of shaker or glass.

Jigger, double headed—the larger part holds either 1 1/2 or 2 oz, the smaller holds either 3/4 or 1 oz.

Bar knife
Can opener
Corkscrew

Bar tongs

Barspoon

Champagne tongs—for removing stubborn corks
Champagne bottle sealer

Cocktail sticks
Cocktail stirrers

Straws

Coasters

Ice bucket
Ice scoop
Ice tongs

Dash bottles–mostly for bitters such as Angostura and orange bitters

Fruit press

Grater

Wooden muddler

Carving board

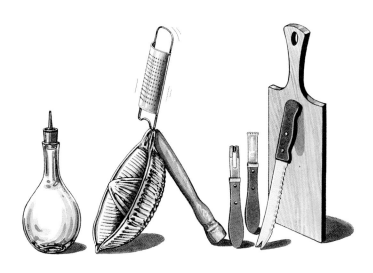

BAR GLASSES Beautifully crafted, simple, economical glasses for the bar are what every bartender wants to have.

Glasses come in the most adventuresome forms, often created by famous glass designers, but these are not suitable for use in the bar.

Required bar glasses:

1) **Aperitif glass**
2) **Port or sherry glass**
3) **Sour glass**
4. **Sparkling wine or Champagne flute**
5) **Cocktail glass**
6) **Martini glass**
7) **Whisky glass, tumbler, or old-fashioned glass**
8) **Small highball glass**
9) **Large highball glass**
10) **Collins glass**
11) **Balloon wine glass**
12) **Irish coffee glass (heat resistant)**
13) **Punch, grog, or toddy glass**
(heat resistant)

1   2   3   4

5

6

7

8

9

10

11

12

13

THE BOTTLES AT THE BAR are the pride and joy of every professional bartender. They are arranged in front and back of the bartender so that they are always within reach and in the same place.

Directly behind each of the most commonly used liquor bottles stands a replacement bottle. Many bars have a cooling trough in the front area where juices and liquors that must be kept cool are stored. A professional bar naturally keeps all the well-known liquors in stock.

The most important mixing liquors are:
- Gin
- Vodka
- Brandy
- Whisk(e)y
- Rum, tequila, cachaça
- Vermouth
- Liqueurs
- Fruit brandies

MIXERS, WATER, AND SODAS
- Tonic water
- Bitter lemon
- Ginger ale
- Seven-Up
- Cola
- Mineral water (still and sparkling)
- Soda water

JUICES AT THE BAR The most important juice at the bar? If I could have only one juice at the bar, it would be **lemon juice** (always fresh squeezed). Without it I wouldn't stand behind any bar in the world however famous it may be! It is the juice of the classic cocktails—the juice of the drink category known as sours. And it is, presumably, the juice that was used at the very dawn of cocktail history.

Gin Fizz, Daiquiri, Whiskey Sour—juiceless and lifeless without fresh-squeezed lemon juice!

Orange juice and lemon juice absolutely must be fresh squeezed.

For those juices that are not fresh squeezed, of course only the best-quality juice should be used, and frozen products are usually better than the others.

Grapefruit juice

Lime juice (Rose's lime juice)

Mango, maracuja (passion fruit), papaya, etc.

Pineapple juice (unsweetened)

Tomato juice (only the very best quality!)

Pour the juice into a bottle and shake it before using!

SUGAR SYRUPS AND FRUIT SYRUPS

Fruit syrups are natural fruit juices from which the sugar has been boiled away, and they are absolutely **essential in mixed drinks** (as a rule, a few drops suffice).

Grenadine syrup: This strong, blood-red grenadine syrup (made from pomegranates) is number one among fruit syrups. For many cocktails it not only constitutes the sweetening part but also gives them color ranging from deep red to pink, depending on the amount that is mixed in.

Sugar syrups (also called gum or sirop de gomme) can easily be made at home: stir sugar into hot water and allow to boil. Skim, allow to cool, and pour into bottles. Store in a cool, dark place. (The ratio of the mix: 1 pound—2⅔ cups—of granulated sugar per cup of water.)

Other syrups:

Almond milk syrup (orgeat)

Banana syrup

Coconut cream

Coconut milk

Cranberry syrup

Lime syrup

Mango syrup

Maple syrup

Maracuja (passion fruit) syrup

Papaya syrup

Peppermint syrup (sirop de menthe)

Raspberry syrup

Sugar cane syrup (sirop de canne)

BITTERS

Angostura bitters—88° proof; the number-one bitters served at the bar. Originally developed as a medicine to fight off malaria by the German military physician Dr. Siegert in the city of Angostura in Venezuela. Angostura is made from herbal extracts. (Along with angostura bark, it contains numerous aromatic plant extracts such as cinnamon, cinchona bark, clove, orange peels, nutmeg, ginger—reportedly over forty ingredients.) The exact measure of ingredients in the blend remains a company secret.

Orange bitters—80° proof; the second-most popular herbal bitters at the bar. It is made from sour orange rinds (from unripened sour oranges) steeped in alcohol (usually gin), without sugar.

Peach bitters—60°–80° proof; an herbal bitters with a peach flavor.

Other bitters:
Apricot bitters
Peychaud bitters (New Orleans)

FRUIT AT THE BAR

Lemons

Limes

Oranges

Pineapples

Cucumbers

and various tropical fruits

GARNISHES FOR THE BAR

Cocktail cherries with stems (maraschino cherries)

Sweet cocktail cherries (amarelle cherries)

Lemon wedges, peels, zest, and spirals

Lime wedges

Orange wedges and orange zest

Pineapple chunks (not canned—I am opposed to all canned fruits. Better none than canned!)

Green olives—use only those soaked in salt water (for Martinis)

Pearl onions (for Gibsons)

Mint (for Juleps and Mojitos)

Celery stalks, peeled (for Virgin Marys and Bloody Marys)

Cucumber peels (for Pimm's)

SPICES, SEASONING SAUCES, AROMATICS

Salt

Pepper

Celery salt

Tabasco

Worcestershire sauce

Fleurs d' orange (orange blossom water, available in apothecaries)

Nutmeg

Clove

Cinnamon

Olive oil

Ketchup

Rose oil

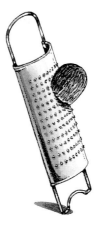

SUGAR, SWEETENERS

Sugar cubes

Powdered sugar

Superfine sugar

Brown sugar

Honey

MISCELLANEOUS

Eggs

Cream

Milk

Dark chocolate

GARNISHING AND DECORATING COCKTAILS AND DRINKS

It is incomprehensible to me that even in cocktail competitions cocktails are garnished and "decorated" as in common chain establishments and that this actually influences the jury. One might assume that the little umbrellas, flags, and spears with fruit pieces are intended to obscure the fact that these drinks are often lousy.

The "creativity" of the mixer knows almost no bounds in the endeavor of cocktail decoration; the bartender may display anything he can think of to toss in. To me, a cocktail is not a fruit or vegetable salad and is not at all suited for little umbrellas or national flags. Those who fear the imagination of such bartenders are forced to order their drinks with "**no vegetables, please.**"

What place do *stuffed* olives have in a Martini?

PRESLICED FRUITS This is a matter of the setting, and in bars that have rush hours, it comes in handy, but . . .

Not long ago I was in a world-famous hotel where I wanted to enjoy a nightcap around midnight. The bartender, already yawning with boredom as he impatiently waited for closing, leaned against a gorgeous bar, which by this time resembled a battlefield after defeat.

Without even seeing the bartender at work, his lack of care and complete indifference in preparing the last cocktails that had been ordered was obvious. There they stood, dull and life-less in their glasses before they even reached the guests.

When I noticed the sticky plastic containers of wrinkled, presliced fruit garnishes that had not survived the evening, I'd had just about enough. I went and had myself a bottle of beer in a corner pizza parlor a few steps away.

TERMINOLOGY

THE MOST IMPORTANT INTERNATIONAL BAR TERMS

After-dinner cocktail—a drink served after a meal

Aperitif—a drink to stimulate the appetite

Bar glass—a mixing or stirring glass

Bar list—the bar menu

Barspoon—a long spoon for stirring drinks in a mixing glass

Bartender—one who mixes and serves drinks at a bar

Before-dinner cocktail—a drink served before a meal

Blend—mixing or combining in liquor production, such as in blending malt whisk(e)y with grain whisk(e)y

Blender—an electric mixer

Boston shaker—an American shaker that consists of a glass and a stainless steel container

Bowl—a metal or glass container

Brand—a particular firm's product

Brut—dry (used for describing Champagne)

Chaser (or filler)—liquid (such as juice, soda) used to fill up or follow a drink

Cordial—liqueur (British and American)

Crusta—a sugar-rimmed glass

Dash—a splash, the smallest bar measure (usually of bitters, syrups, or liqueurs)

Decant—to pour an old wine that has deposits into another container, most often done with red and fortified wines (vintage port)

Digestif—a drink served after dinner

Flavoring agent—a cocktail ingredient such as syrup or bitters

Float—a very small amount, usually of liquor, that is carefully poured on top of a cocktail (such as pouring some brandy into a Champagne Julep)

Frosted glass—a frozen glass (such as a cocktail glass)

Grind—to pulverize or grate (such as nutmeg)

Magnum—a double-sized bottle

Millésime (French)—vintage Champagne

Mixing glass—a stirring glass

Modifier—a cocktail ingredient (such as liquor, juice, syrup)

Muddler—a mortar and pestle for muddling sugar cubes with herbs or limes, etc. (Caipirinha)

Neat—unmixed

On the rocks—with ice cubes

Plain (neat)—without anything (such as whisk(e)y plain)

Prechilled glasses—glasses chilled ahead of time (for Martinis, for example)

Proof—American data about alcohol content (for example 100° proof is 50 percent alcohol by volume)

Salt rim—glass rimmed with salt

Sec—dry (description applied to wine, etc.)

Sediment—deposits in old wine (vintage port, etc.)

Short drink—drink served in a small glass (2–3 oz)

Sparkling water—carbonated water

Squeezer—a fruit press

Straight up—unmixed, without ice

Sugar rim—glass rimmed with sugar

Sundries—bar tidbits such as nuts, popcorn, crackers

Tall drink—a drink served in a tall glass (5 oz or more)

Tumbler—a stemless whisk(e)y glass

Twist (lemon, orange)—a small piece of peel that is squeezed over a drink

Vintage—description of the year a product is made (for port, Champagne)

Zest—a small piece of the colored part of a lemon or orange peel

SALT OR SUGAR RIMS Moisten the rim of a cocktail glass—for a salt rim use a lemon wedge, for a sugar rim use an orange wedge. Then turn the glass into a saucer filled with salt or sugar. (For guests who order their drink with a salt or sugar rim, I leave a small part of the rim clear for sipping.)

THE BARTENDER

EDUCATION Bartending is an attractive profession; it is nevertheless difficult to interest young people in pursuing it beyond practicing their magic behind the bar for a short time.

Let it be said: As in other professions, without education there's no success!

A bartender's education is typically only part of the training to be a waiter in hotel bars. Unfortunately, there are hardly any famous independent bars in which one can learn the profession in depth. Bartending schools provide nothing more than a theoretical familiarity.

I am often asked how long it takes until one can mix drinks expertly.

A famous cocktail recipe book from the 1950s says that nothing can go too terribly awry if the recipes are followed precisely and if top-quality ingredients are used to begin with (which should be a matter of course in a good bar). There is nothing really untrue about this statement, but even so it's not so simple!

Mixing drinks well is only *part* of what it takes to be a good bartender.

ADVANCED TRAINING A solid technical knowledge and interest in continual improvement are basic requirements. Modesty, too, is required when it comes to creating new cocktails, because in truth there is hardly anything new to create. Anyone who concocts new drinks would do well to look regularly in cocktail recipe books. Most will discover that their newest sensation has already appeared in one place or another.

A beginner who wants to develop expertise should most definitely travel to other countries, even if that means earning much less pay.

As in almost no other profession, bartending presents enormous possibilities to gain worldwide experience.

A bartender should speak several foreign languages to be able to deal with an international public.

LIFESTYLE FOR THE PROFESSION The work of a bartender usually means night work! Thus physically it's very challenging. Without being in good physical and mental condition, it's hard to take. That's why the lifestyle for the profession also means: no alcohol during work!

I can remember some excellent bartenders who did not heed this basic rule—most are no longer working in the profession.

THE WORKPLACE There are times in a bar when the bartender has to work as though on an assembly line. To survive, he must have a fully equipped and perfectly organized workplace. That's the only way he can maintain good spirits and a pleasant mood. Clean clothes should be a matter of course. And the bartender should not smoke or drink anything at the bar.

THE BARTENDER AS TRAINER The ideal way for young people to begin their training is in a good bar with a barkeeper who sets an example.

In every bar it is imperative to have experienced bartenders who take responsibility and know the guests. They bring stability to the bar—especially on less harmonious evenings.

Young people are an absolute necessity in any good bar. Without fresh, unjaded young people who are eager to learn there is no impetus to stave off monotony and a dull routine—things come to a standstill, as any good trainer knows.

DEALING WITH THE PUBLIC The bartender is neither emcee nor circus director.

He should be a quiet, reserved advisor who leads—but never misleads—his guests, and who never serves them too much. If a bartender respects his guests, they will respect him too.

Overfamiliarity undermines this!

The bartender knows his regular guests and their customary drinks. He must also know his way around difficult drinks. And that requires many years of experience.

Discreetly the bartender lets the undesirable guest know that this is not the place for him.

He does not encourage his guests to order the most expensive drinks; he is careful not to let them drink indiscriminately; and he assesses their financial situation and tolerance level for alcohol. He is more than merely an expert drink mixer—he is a host to genial guests, a tamer of brutish guests, and a therapist to the melancholy.

THE BAR OWNER A bar can function only when the proprietor has succeeded in building a good team. This is possible only if the owner and the crew have mutual respect. Seldom is the fame of a bar due exclusively to its proprietor. The best situation is when the owner too has personal experience working behind the bar.

A bar can and certainly should earn money, but it would be a mistake to believe that owning a bar means easy money. A bar has a social and cultural function as well.

EPILOGUE

More than twenty years in the bar business—more than half of them at Schumann's—and two bar books about cocktails with bartending anecdotes.

And now a third book—finally "my book," the one I would have wished to have and read when I began my training in the profession.

I have tried to write a kind of bartending bible of interest to beginners in the profession, to those interested in bars, and I hope also to professionals.

As our century comes to a close, cocktails and drinks are once again popular. Indeed they never entirely disappeared, although there were years in which they sank into oblivion. Certainly some of the fashionable cocktails of today will one day be stricken from the bar lists; however, I am convinced that a few of them will become classics and go down in history. I would be very proud if only a handful came from our bar.

DRINKING AT THE BAR When I began my career as a barkeeper some twenty years ago, cocktails had fallen out of fashion and nearly become a lost art.

I worked behind the bar of a well-known establishment, and of course we had a menu listing the current international cocktails. But every evening only a handful of them, and always the same ones, were ordered, and most were chosen only for their color. Since then a lot has changed, and to the happiness of all good bartenders, the number of cocktail customers has grown ever larger.

That is why now more than ever it is important to lead the cocktail drinker in the right direction! A bartender who serves his evening guests cocktails of all kinds—from sweet to dry, whisk(e)y-based and then gin-based—is a bungler.

Of course a large number of bar guests prefer their drinks neat. However, I do not believe that there is a single person who formed an immediate liking for a liquor after first tasting it neat—except for some Irishmen and Scots who maintain that they were born into the world with a glass of whisk(e)y.

Cognac and whisk(e)y taste terrible on the very first sip. If, however, one is properly introduced to enjoying drinks neat, they can provide a lifetime of pleasure. One discovers which liquors comfort, invigorate, or support—in bad times or good. And only in a few cases is one persuaded to change.

All professional drinkers have their liquors! Whether liquors are enjoyed neat or as cocktails, a bartender or bar waiter should try to lead his regular guests in the right direction. No respected bar would serve its guests too many drinks! The support of civilized drinking is what makes a bar fun and brings it the highest esteem.

Charles Schumann

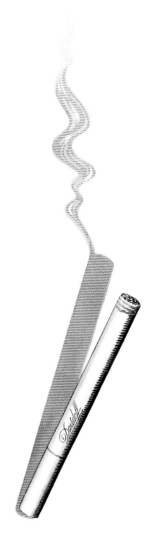

Acknowledgments

When I began compiling this book, I had no idea what effort and work lay before me. Now that the editing has come to an end, I must say that without help and support I don't believe this book, which is so important to me, would have ever come to pass.

Special thanks go to my coworker, Bärbel Lamprechter, who from the very first line deciphered my notes, wrote revisions over the years, wrote and rewrote—in many hours of her free time—and never grew impatient through it all.

Above all I would like to thank Stefan Gabányi, who spent much time and effort in the final months before the book was completed checking merchandise information, organizing the text, and helping write revisions. Without his work and his knowledge the book would not have lived up to my expectations.

Thanks go also to thank Karl Rudolf, a journalist, who in the very last moments offered to look over the merchandise information once more, to expand and correct it.

I would also like to thank my editor, Ria Lottermoser, above all for supporting Günter Mattei and believing that this book would someday be finished, and who again and again persuasively conveyed this to the publisher.

This book is inconceivable without Günter Mattei. He not only gave it his artistic handiwork, but also through his knowledge of our earlier collaborations fundamentally contributed to creating a bar book comprehensible to everyone.

BIBLIOGRAPHY

Bespaloff, Alexis. *Alexis Bespaloff's Complete Guide to Wine.* New York: Penguin Books, 1994.

Blue, Anthony Dias. *The Complete Book of Mixed Drinks.* New York: HarperCollins, 1993.

Brandl, Franz. *Gourmet Mix Guide.* Zurich, Edition Willsberger, 1982.

Cotton, Leo. *Mr. Boston Official Bartender's Guide.* Revised and updated by Elin McCoy and John Frederick Walker. New York: Warner Books, 1988.

Craddock, Harry. *The Savoy Cocktail Book.* London: Constable and Company, 1930.

Faith, Nicolas. *Cognac.* Boston: David R. Godine, 1987.

Grossman, Harold. *Grossman's Guide to Wines, Beers, and Spirits.* Revised by Harriet Lembeck. New York: Charles Scribner's Sons, 1983.

Hallgarten, Peter. *Spirits and Liqueurs.* London: Faber and Faber, 1983.

Jackson, Michael. *The World Guide to Whisky.* London: Dorling Kindersley, 1987.

——. *The Pocket Bartender's Guide.* New York: Simon and Schuster, 1979.

Regan, Gary. *The Bartender's Bible.* New York: HarperCollins, 1991.

Stevenson, Tom. *Champagne.* London: Sotheby's Publications, 1986.

Schumann, Charles. *Schumann's Barbuch.* Munich: Heyne, 1984.

——. *Tropical Bar Book.* New York: Stewart, Tabori and Chang, 1989. Originally published as *Schumann's Tropical Barbuch.* by Heyne, Munich, 1986.

INDEX

Translated from the German by Laura Lindgren

EDITOR: FRAU RIA LOTTERMOSER
DESIGNERS: GÜNTER MATTEI AND JOSEF SCHAAF

English-language edition
EDITOR: JACQUELINE DECTER
DESIGNER: LAURA LINDGREN
EDITORIAL CONSULTANTS: ELIN MCCOY
AND JOHN FREDERICK WALKER
PRODUCTION EDITOR: OWEN DUGAN
PRODUCTION MANAGER: LOU BILKA

First published in the United States of America in 1995 by
Abbeville Press, 116 West 23rd Street, New York, N.Y. 10011.
First published in Germany in 1991 by
Wilhelm Heyne Verlag GmbH & Co., KG, Munich.

Copyright © 1991 by Wilhelm Heyne Verlag GmbH & Co. KG
English translation copyright © 1995 Abbeville Press, Inc.

First edition
17 19 21 23 25 24 22 20 18 16

Library of Congress Cataloging-in-Publication Data
Schumann, Charles.
   American bar : the artistry of mixing drinks / Charles Schumann :
illustrated by Günter Mattei : translated from the German by Laura
Lindgren.
        p.   cm.
   Includes bibliographical references and index.
   ISBN 1-55859-853-7
   1. Bartending. 2. Cocktails. I. Title.
   TX951.S424   1995
   641.8'74–dc20   95-21222